KATAHDIN

**A Guide to Baxter Park
& Katahdin**

KATAHDIN

A Guide to Baxter Park & Katahdin

STEPHEN CLARK

North Country Press • Unity, Maine

Library of Congress Cataloging in Publication Data

Clark, Stephen.
Katahdin: a guide to Baxter Park & Katahdin.

Bibliography: p. 89
Includes index.
1. Hiking — Maine — Baxter State Park — Guide-books.
2. Trails — Maine — Baxter State Park — Guide-books.
3. Baxter State Park (Me.) — Guide books.   I. Title.
GV199.42.M22B383   1985   917.41   85-2843
ISBN 0-945980-00-0 (soft) North Country Press

Updated for third printing, April, 1988.
Published by North Country Press, Unity, Maine 04988.
Printed in the United States of America.
Book and cover design by Abby Trudeau.
Special thanks to Patti Bouchard and Bonnie Collins of the
Maine State Library.
Cover photo by Lester Kenway.
All photographs in this publication are cour-
tesy of the Avery Collection, Maine State
Library.

The works of men are short lived. Monuments decay, buildings crumble and wealth vanishes, but Katahdin in its massive grandeur will forever remain the mountain of the people of Maine.

PERCIVAL PROCTER BAXTER

Contents

Included with this *Guide* is the up to date, four-color topographical map *BAXTER PARK AND KATAHDIN*. This shows all trails, campgrounds, roads, important points of interest, as well as all natural features.

Extra copies may be obtained from the Baxter State Park Authority, the Publisher (North Country Press, Unity, Maine 04988), or mountaineering supply concerns.

PREFACE

Baxter State Park and Katahdin are unique natural features not only of Maine, but the Northeastern United States. Surprisingly, prior to the printing of this guide, there was no comprehensive guide for people who were interested in exploring the Park's wonders, or wanted a general informational source about the Park.

There has been an exceptional amount of writing about Katahdin and the Park, particularly romances, histories, and journals of expeditions to the area, but not in a condensed form for the casual visitor. In the past 30 years two trail guides have been used. The best was the Maine Appalachian Trail Club's *Katahdin Section* (of the Appalachian Trail). The other is the Appalachian Mountain Club's description of the Park's trails in their *Maine Mountain Guide*.

The *Katahdin Section* gradually became outdated and obsolete until its discontinuance in 1975. The *Maine Mountain Guide*, although modern and up-to-date, is limited in its ability to deal in depth with the Park because of its comprehensive nature in describing all Maine's mountains.

It is the author's intention to provide a guide to the Park that will not only give the visitor a description of its many outstanding features, but general information on history, geology, wildlife, how the Park came into existence, and other pertinent information. Its emphasis will be on descriptions of the trail system that lead to the Park's features.

The author has utilized many sources of information for this guide. The most important were back issues of the M.A.T.C.'s *Katahdin Section Guide*, previously mentioned. Myron Avery, a native of Lubec, Maine, and a past chairman of the Appalachian Trail Conference before his death in 1952, carefully researched histories about the Park and authored much of that Guide. He also compiled *An Annotated Bibliography of Katahdin* (with Edward S.C. Smith) which was last published by the Appalachian Trail Conference in 1950. This is now out of print.

In 1976, the author spent a most enjoyable summer in measuring the Park's trails with a wheel and compiling data for new trails added in recent years. He, like many others, became deeply infatuated with the Park. It is his hope that this guide will be of some help to the reader in discovering those features within the Park which will provide a most memorable experience.

Acknowledgments

The author owes much to the many people who advised or aided in the gathering of information and writing of this guide.

In particular, Park Rangers, Tom Chase, his father Roger Chase, Ivan Roy, and Bernard Crabtree aided the author in the many days needed to collect trail data. Park supervisor Irvin "Buzz" Caverly at the Millinocket Office checked many of the facts pertaining to overall Park operations. Lester Kenway, the Park's Trail Supervisor, provided much of the trail data for new trails that have been added in the Park since 1978.

Leroy Dudley Cross of Brunswick, long time contributor to many New England mountaineering and hiking books and periodicals, checked for accuracy and correct usage of mountaineering terms.

So all of you, for better or worse, are now a part of this Guide.

STEPHEN CLARK

I

ABOUT THE PARK

BAXTER PARK is owned by the people of the State of Maine. The circumstances by which they came into possession of this land and its natural wonders are unusual, with few parallels in the history of our country. (See section on "How the Park Came to Be.") It is administered by a State agency known as the Baxter State Park Authority. This body is made up of three members: the State of Maine Attorney General, the Director of the Bureau of Forestry (formerly the Forest Commissioner), and the Commissioner of Inland Fisheries and Wildlife. When these positions are appointed by the Governor (the Legislature appoints the Attorney General), they automatically become members of the Authority. The Authority is somewhat autonomous from other State agencies and is not under the direct authority of the Governor or Legislature of the State.

The Authority in turn appoints a Supervisor who is responsible for the hiring of Park personnel, long range planning, and who serves as chief administrator of the Park.

THE PARK AS A WILDERNESS

In accepting the Park as a gift from Percival P. Baxter, the State agreed to maintain and protect it in the condition that the donor wished. There are many deeds of trust, Legislative Acts, and expressions of philosophy contained in correspondence which explicitly direct how the Park is to be managed and used.

Craft called bateaux were used for water transportation in the early days.

First: The Park should remain in its "natural wild state," essentially a wilderness, and that the forests of the Park were not to be harvested for commercial purposes. This stipulation does not apply to parts of two townships in the northern part of the Park which could be used for "scientific forestry."

Second: The Park should remain as a "sanctuary for wild birds and beasts," essentially a wildlife sanctuary. There are two parcels of land within the park which are excluded from this requirement: a small section near the southeast corner of the Park, and a larger one north of the Perimeter Road in the northern part of the Park.

Third: The Park can be used for limited recreational purposes such as hiking, camping, fishing, picnicking, photography, or canoeing. Forms of recreation which include the use of motorized devices are excluded as they are incompatible with a wilderness. Cars are allowed on the Perimeter Road and several short spurs of this road.

Visitors to the Park should carefully note that **recreational uses are subordinate to the prime objective of maintaining the Park in its "natural wild state."** This may be translated into rules such as limiting the number of people in the Park, excluding pets, or maintaining only primitive facilities.

The management of a park for wilderness values first, and recreational uses second, is the **exact opposite** of all other State Parks in Maine. In those parks the main purpose is to maximize a variety of recreational opportunities for park visitors. Therefore, visitors to Baxter Park must make this distinction in their understanding of how the Park is operated, and particularly in their behavior at the Park.

The Park is mainly used in the summer, although in recent years more people are using the Park in winter. The Park opens in mid-May and closes in mid-October. Not all the campgrounds are open for this full period. The Baxter Park rules and regulations, published yearly, will give an exact listing of opening and closing dates of each campground.

There are special rules which govern winter use of the Park.

If winter climbing is contemplated, stringent rules about quali-
fications, equipment, and back-up protection must be followed.

THE PARK AS A RECREATIONAL EXPERIENCE

Baxter is different from other parks. And because it is different,
it requires different behavior from its visitors.

First: Much of the park is as close to a true wilderness as most
of us will experience, unless we travel to the wilds of Canada.
The visitor must limit his or her activities so as not to detract
from the wilderness itself or the wilderness experience sought by
others.

Peace, quiet, solitude, serenity, and pure enjoyment of natural beauty are the human values associated with a wilderness experience. Loud radios, motor boats, tv's, parties, hurrying, or
crowds are not synonymous with values to be sought at Baxter.
There may be times when crowds and noise must be tolerated,
but they are not what people come to Baxter to discover.

Second: Because large numbers of people will destroy the
very thing one comes to find, this means numbers must be limited. Therefore, in peak periods of recreational activity (July-
August) some may be disappointed in not gaining admittance to
the Park, or being unable to camp at their favorite spot if they
are admitted.

Third: Because the environment of a wilderness park is most
difficult to manage and maintain, each visitor will be subjected
to a degree of regulation in his activities not found in other
parks. People who are accustomed to the freedom of going
where they want when they want, as in the White Mts. or at
Acadia, will rasp somewhat at Baxter's more regulated activities. It is hoped that the visitor, after some initial adjustment,
will recognize the reasons for the restrictions and cooperate in
maintaining the objectives for which they were established.

Fourth: It is hoped that the visitor will be able to leave the

Park enriched by his or her experiences with the natural world that so many of our generation seek, but so few find.

THE PARK AS A WILDLIFE SANCTUARY

The conveyances of land to the State by Percival Baxter contain a provision that the area shall be kept in a "natural wild state and as a **sanctuary for wild beasts and birds**" and that trapping and hunting are not permitted. In 1921, ten years before Baxter first purchased the property, the Maine Legislature designated part of this area as a game preserve. There are however, two parts of the Park where this stipulation does not apply.

Hunting and trapping are permitted on a small area in the southeast part of the Park, in Township 2, Range 9. This area is roughly around Abol Pond, Rum Brook, and Togue Pond. A much larger area is located in the northern part of the Park and is roughly north of the Perimeter Road in parts of T6 R10 and T5 R9. For the exact location of these areas, see the map "Baxter Park and Katahdin." All hunting in permitted areas is subject to the general laws and regulations governing hunting and trapping published by the State Bureau of Inland Fisheries and Wildlife.

For the bulk of the Park, the opportunity to observe deer, moose, black bear, and other wild animals in their native habitat is one of the high points of a trip to the Park.

The actual wording which conveys the designation of the Park as a wildlife sanctuary is important and is quoted here (Ch. 2, Private and Special Laws, 1955, approved January 18, 1955, by the Legislature).

SANCTUARY FOR WILD BEASTS AND BIRDS

The State is authorized to maintain the balance of nature among the different species of wildlife; to control disease and epidemics of the wildlife of the Park. Such control shall be exercised by the Baxter State Park Authority. The destruction of any species of wildlife shall be carried on exclusively by the Personnel of said Authority and of the Forest and Fish and Game Departments.

All work carried on by the State in connection with the above shall be in accordance with the best forestry and wildlife practices and shall be undertaken having in mind that the sole purpose of the donor in creating this Park is to protect the forests and wildlife therein as a great wilderness area unspoiled by Man. Nothing shall be done for the purpose of obtaining income but should there be incidental income it is to be used solely for the care, operation and protection of this Wilderness area.

HOW THE PARK CAME TO BE

Baxter Park and the natural wonders contained within its boundaries have been set aside from commercial use and development. The Park has been reserved to be maintained for the most part as a wilderness environment similar to that which pre-dated the arrival of Europeans in Maine (approx. 1620–1750). It has been reserved as a wildlife sanctuary and for the recreational use of the people of Maine and their guests.

The land that comprises Baxter Park, approximately 201,018 acres or over 314 square miles, was not acquired with public funds, state or federal. Nor was it "excess land" originally in the public domain and simply designated as a park as was the case with most of our Federal parks and forests.

Rather, it was the **gift of one man** to the people of his state.

Percival Proctor Baxter was born into a well-to-do Portland, Maine, family on November 22, 1876. He was well educated, and ran successfully for the legislature in 1905, at the age of 29. He became Governor of the State in 1920 and retired from political office in 1925. During this period he became intensely interested in forming a public preserve centered around Katahdin.

Katahdin offers some spectacular views.

His efforts to convince the legislature to commit the State to acquire lands and form a new park met with repeated failure. The legislature frowned on the acquisition of recreational lands for a predominantly (at that time) rural population and because of powerful opposition from timber and landholding interests. During the period between 1925 and 1930, Baxter decided to raise the money through wise investments in stocks and bonds and do privately what he could not do publicly.

In late 1930 Baxter acquired title to about 6,000 acres of land composing most of the main massif of Katahdin. In 1931 he offered the land to the State as a gift.

Thus started the remarkable story of how the Park came to be. There are several histories of subsequent additions to the Park, but a most interesting account is in Baxter's own words in a speech given just prior to 1944.

THE PURCHASE OF THE LAND
By Former Governor Percival P. Baxter

In 1905 at the age of twenty-nine as one of the younger members of the State Legislature, I began to learn something of my native State, its people, its resources, its wildlife, and its possibilities for the future. It was not, however, until 1917 that I attempted to induce the State Legislature to acquire by purchase the mountainous region around Mt. Katahdin.

For eight years, both as a legislator and as Governor, I worked unceasingly to secure legislation for the establishment of a State Park at Katahdin to be held as a great primitive recreational area and wildlife sanctuary, but the opposition proved too strong and the legislators of those days were not interested. During the years 1917 to 1925, time after time, my State Park plans were defeated.

In 1925, those who opposed me no doubt felt relieved when I retired from the Governorship to private life. But oftentimes defeats later turn into victories, and so it was in this Park project. After leaving the Governor's office I gave up all thought of securing any park legislation and determined to buy the land myself and give it to the State. It is interesting to observe that the very people who, while I was in office, were my strongest opponents later became my firm friends.

When I went to these land owners, asking them to sell me their lands, they treated me courteously and fairly. They told me that while they did not care to sell their lands they would do so because they had come to realize that I was trying to do something worthwhile for Maine. These land owners have shown a remarkably fine spirit, and I want the people of Maine to know how splendidly they have cooperated with me in selling me their forest lands.

Up to the time my first purchase of 6,000 acres was made in 1930, I never had owned any forest or timber land. My Park started from absolutely nothing, and every acre has been bought since 1930. Today the land acquired for the State totals 114,040 acres or 178 square miles all in one piece and comprising almost five townships. A township in Maine, roughly speaking, contains 36 square miles.

For all practical purposes, after twenty-seven years of effort, the Park is complete. Maybe, however, I shall be able to enlarge it from time to time for there are several areas it would be well to acquire. The Park stands right in the center of the northern portion of our State, a wild mountainous country now forever set aside and held in trust by the State as a public park, forest reserve, and wildlife sanctuary for present and future generations of Maine people. The State Legislature very generously has named this area Baxter State Park.

The distance from Portland to the summit of Mt. Katahdin is 250 miles. There are several foot trails leading to the summit, and a rough but passable motor road passes through the westerly portion of the Park. All along the way there are grand views of Katahdin and the other thirty peaks within the Park area. This district is typical of the wild lands of Maine. It has within its borders lakes, swamps, beaver dams, rivers, mountains, good timber lands and burnt-over lands, meadows, and boulders in profusion. Moose, deer, wildcats, bears, foxes, and all the smaller animals and birds abound therein. All these creatures are safe from the hunters, and the sound of the axe and of falling trees never will echo through these forests. Katahdin always should and must remain the wild, storm-swept, untouched-by-man region it now is; that is its great charm. Only small cabins for mountain climbers and those who love the wilderness should be allowed there, only trails for those who travel on foot or horseback, a place where nature rules and where the creatures of the forest hold undisputed dominion.

This area was donated to the State on three conditions: first, it shall be held by the State in trust forever; second, that it shall be used for public parks, forests, and recreation; third, that it shall ever be kept in its natural wild state and as a sanctuary for wild beasts and birds.

A map published by the Appalachian Mountain Club records that there are more than 30 different mountain peaks within this area.

A modern civilization with its trailers and gasoline fumes, its unsightly billboards, its radio and jazz, encroaches on the Maine wilderness. The time yet may come when only the Katahdin region remains undefiled by man. To acquire this Katahdin region for the people of Maine has been undertaken by me as my life's work, and I hope as the years roll on that this State Park will be enjoyed by an ever-increasing number of Maine people and by those who come to us from beyond our borders.

Katahdin, 5,267 feet, stands above the surrounding plain unique in grandeur and glory. The works of men are short-lived. Monuments decay, buildings crumble, and wealth vanishes, but Katahdin in its massive grandeur will forever remain the mountain of the people of Maine. Throughout the ages it will stand as an inspiration to the men and women of this State.

In 1944 Baxter had acquired and deeded to the State 114,040 acres of land. After this date he continued the process of buying tracts, small and large, adding them to the Park.

At the age of 83, 18 years after his address, Baxter acquired the last parcel, a 7,764 acre tract in the southern part of the Park around Abol and Togue Ponds. The final acreage stands at 201,018, over 314 square miles. It took him 37 years from the time he retired as governor to acquire the present Park acreage.

There were 32 separate parcels varying in size from 136 acres to a prodigous 25,025 acres, one entire township in the northern part of the Park. Some of these parcels were bought with the right of the former owner (usually a timber producing company) to harvest timber until a later date. The last of those rights expired in 1973, so the State owns all rights to the entire Park (excluding certain water rights on Webster and Matagamon Lakes).

Some of the last acquisitions given to the State were not donated to be managed under the "forever wild" stipulation. An area of 28,534 acres, about 14% of the total Park land, was designated by Baxter to be used for "scientific forestry practices." This land can be harvested in a manner similar to other commercial timberlands but with the additional objectives in a manner of allowing experimentation and providing understanding and information rather than profit, although financial gain from the sale of timber is allowed. This area is generally located between the Perimeter Road and the north and west Park boundaries (all of T6 R10 and part of T6 R9).

Baxter decided to deviate from the "forever wild" concept for two reasons. First, he had occasion to visit several intensively managed European forests which greatly impressed him. The more orderly management techniques were in graphic contrast to the "cut and run" practices followed by Maine companies at that time. He saw an opportunity to improve forestry practices which would result in long-term benefits to Maine people.

Second, there were concerns at that time that too much land was being removed from timber production, which could result in substantial economic hardship to his Maine people.

Thus, the "scientific forestry" areas of the Park were attempts to compromise his earlier views with newer outlooks. This points to Baxter as a man who was not locked into one rigid point of view. He was a man, even in his later years, who was concerned with people's welfare and was willing to modify his views for their benefit.

Baxter also modified his earlier "wildlife sanctuary" concept on several of his last donations to the State. This was done to placate some of the resentment of hunting interests who in the past had gained their livelihood from hunting or providing for hunters on what is now Park lands. There are two main areas open to hunting: an area north of the Perimeter Road (most of T6 R10 and T6 R9) and the 7,764 acre tract at the very south end of the Park around Togue and Abol Ponds.

In the later years before Baxter's death, he concentrated on providing a continuing income to administer the Park after his death. A trust fund was formed through a prominent Boston banking firm so that income derived from the fund could be used to operate the Park. This income, plus nominal fees collected from visitors to the Park, are the only sources of Park operating funds. No tax monies are used for the Park's operation, although some State funds are used to maintain the Park's Perimeter Road.

Baxter died in 1969 at the age of 90. He is best known for the gift of the Park but he was also active in other philanthropic causes such as the Baxter School for the Deaf near Portland. He was a proud man who wanted to be recognized for his deeds. The sum total of his lifetime would indicate a deep commitment to his fellow man. And only time will prove how great was his gift to the people of his State.

II

GETTING TO THE PARK

THERE IS ONLY one Trail, one canoe route, and three auto roads that lead into the Park. The trail and canoe routes into and within the Park are dealt with elsewhere in this book. This section is meant to provide information on how to get to the Park by car.

The three car routes are:

Via Millinocket — by far the most popular

Via Greenville — a longer, scenic route

Via Patten — access to the north part of the Park

These three approach routes are described below.

ROAD APPROACHES TO KATAHDIN & BAXTER PARK

To Millinocket

There are two routes to reach the town of Millinocket. The first is by Interstate 95 through Bangor and reaching Millinocket off the **Medway Exit**.

This route has the advantage of an Interstate highway almost to Millinocket. It is somewhat tedious travel and is less scenic than other routes. It is a good route during inclement weather or when time is a factor. Bangor, a city of 40,000, is a good stopping place. There are many restaurants, of both high quality and fast-food types.

Leave Interstate 95 at the **Medway Exit** and proceed west 11 mi. further to Millinocket.

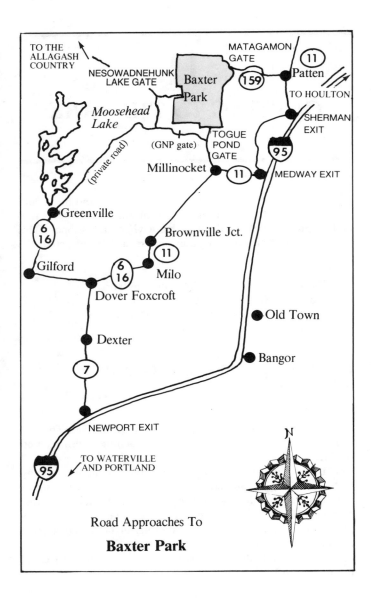

Road Approaches To

Baxter Park

Boston to Millinocket	306 mi. (5½ hr.)
Kittery (N.H. border) to Millinocket	246 mi. (4½ hr.)
Portland to Millinocket	203 mi. (3¾ hr.)
Augusta to Millinocket	146 mi. (3 hr.)
Bangor to Millinocket	70 mi. (1¼ hr.)

A second, more scenic route using Interstate 95 leaves it further south at the **Newport Exit** (west of Bangor) and proceeds north on routes 7, 6, and 11 through the towns of Corinna, Dexter, Dover-Foxcroft, Milo, and Brownville Jct. From Newport to Millinocket it is 81 mi., 15 mi. shorter than using the Interstate all the way to Medway. The small towns and old farms offer the traveler a route with a much greater variety of scenery than the Interstate.

There are a number of small restaurants in these towns, notably in Dover-Foxcroft and Milo.

Millinocket

The town of Millinocket is located 17 mi. south of the Park. The Great Northern Paper Company has a large mill west of the town, and another in East Millinocket. The G.N.P. operations dominate the economy of the area.

The town has a full range of services such as restaurants, motels, garages, laundromats, a small hospital, a small airport, and numerous stores. Visitors from metropolitan areas should be forewarned that business owners close up early and 24-hour service is not available. Cars should definitely be fueled here as there is no gas available at the Park.

Baxter Park Headquarters is located 1 mi. east of the town along Route 11. A visitor's information center is provided here with picnic facilities adjacent to the building.

From Millinocket to the Park (17 mi.)

From Millinocket, the Park Road is followed north toward the prominent peaks of Katahdin. The small settlement of Millinocket Lake is reached 9 mi. from Millinocket. Here is a small store with a gas pump, a recreational campground, and a public beach on the lakeshore. Telephone and power lines end here. There is a float plane service located to the left (west).

From Millinocket Lake it is 6½ mi. to an important fork. **The Park Road turns right,** and onto a gravel road. To the left the surfaced road continues to Abol Bridge over the Penobscot West Branch, then to Ripogenus Dam, loops south, and eventually reaches the town of Greenville 58 mi. from this point.

From the fork, follow the gravel road and in 1½ mi. reach Togue Pond. Here are located private camps and a campground with 30 tent sites. Continue on road and at 17 mi. from Millinocket reach the south entrance to the Park at **Togue Pond Gate.**

Another less-used entrance is reached from Millinocket, but requires longer travel over private, sometimes rough, gravel roads. This is the Nesowadnehunk Lake Gate, located on the Park's west side. Visitors who wish to use this gate should check at the Baxter State Park Headquarters in Millinocket as this gate is not open full time.

Access to the gate requires the traveler to pass through a Great Northern Paper Co. control gate at the Abol Bridge, over the West Branch of the Penobscot. A fee is charged to use this private road. Exact directions to reach the gate can be obtained from the gatekeeper.

Via Patten

The gateway to the northern part of the Park is through the town of Patten. This is a small town located to the east of the Park, 95 mi. north of Bangor. To reach Patten, follow Interstate 95 north of Bangor to the **Sherman Exit,** then follow Route 159 and 11 north about eight mi. further to the town.

Patten is a small farming community located in the midst of the potato-growing belt of Southern Aroostook County. It has garages, several motels, a laundromat, and the usual stores found in a small town. On the outskirts of town is located the **Lumberman's Museum,** a must for any person interested in the history of the Park and how lumbermen lived. It has outstanding displays of equipment, including an old Lombard Steam

Tractor, numerous models of old lumber camps, and a complete sawmill. Allow several hours to adequately see the museum.

From Patten (**you should fuel car here**) take Route 159 NW 10 mi. to Shin Pond. Here is a float-plane base and a small store. Beyond this point the road is private but open to the public. It is

Logging was allowed before the creation of the Park.

known locally as the Grand Lake Road. Grand Lake refers to Matagamon Lake.

At 16 mi. from Patten, cross the Seboeis River, with a picnic site attractively located along the river's bank. At 23 mi. the road begins a long descent into the Penobscot East Branch valley. Excellent views of the Traveler and the mountains in the northern part of the Park are seen.

At 26 mi. reach the bridge crossing the East Branch of the Penobscot River. To the right is a small store (with gas pump) and a private campground. Just across the bridge to the right is a road leading 0.6 mi. to the Grand Lake Dam (owned by Bangor Hydro-Electric Co.). This is a favorite starting point for canoe trips down the rugged East Branch, with its many rapids and falls.

The road then turns north, following the shore of Matagamon Lake, passing close to the sheer cliffs of Horse Mt. to the left.

At 27 mi. from Patten, reach the Matagamon Gate, the northern entrance to the Park.

Via Greenville

A longer, but much more scenic approach to the Park, is through the town of Greenville. This town is reached by **leaving Interstate 95 at Newport,** then following routes 7, 23, and 6 through the towns of Dexter (turn left onto Route 23), Sangerville, Guilford, and Monson. It is 54 mi. from Newport to Greenville.

Greenville is a small town located at the southern end of Moosehead Lake. It is the jumping-off place for the North Maine woods. It has garages, a laundromat, overnight lodging, several restaurants, and stores. D.T. Sanders Store, an old-time canoe trip outfitter, makes an interesting stop. Several large float-plane services are located here. In fact, Greenville is the largest float-plane base in New England. Bush pilots fly patrons to all parts of the Maine woods and north into Canada.

Gas and supplies should be obtained here as this is the "last stop."

From Greenville an unnumbered, but surfaced road is followed north, paralleling the east shore of Moosehead Lake. Ten miles north of Greenville is **Lily Bay State Park**, which is a good overnight stop in approaching Baxter Park. Full camping facilities are available here. The park is attractively located on the east shore of Moosehead Lake.

The small settlement (with one store) of Kokadjo is passed 19 mi. north of Greenville. From this point the road is a private, graveled lumber road open to public use. This is slow going as the road is not maintained for high speed operation.

At 40 mi. north of Greenville pass on left a side road leading to Chesuncook Landing on the shore of that lake. This is a starting point for canoe trips into the North Country and the Allagash Region. Two miles further is Ripogenus Dam, a huge hydroelectric and water-control dam built and operated by the Great Northern Paper Co. From this point the road swings east and follows the Penobscot West Branch downstream.

The road in this area is utilized by huge lumber trucks carrying mammoth loads of logs bound for the mill in Millinocket. **Exercise caution.**

At 54 mi. from Greenville the road crosses the West Branch on Abol Bridge. A beautiful view of Katahdin is seen to the NE. Just across the bridge is a small store and gas pump. A small tenting campground is also located on a point of land formed by the confluence of the Penobscot and Abol Stream. The Appalachian Trail also utilizes this bridge to cross the Penobscot.

Bear left onto a surfaced road. To right is a part of the "Golden Road," a specially-designed lumber road for the huge trucks used by G.N.P. This road is normally not open for public use.

At 58 mi. from Greenville, reach the Baxter Park Road (graveled) **to left.** Ahead, road leads 15 mi. to Millinocket. From this point it is 2 mi. to the Togue Pond Gate House, the southern entrance to the Park. There is a small private campground on the shore of Togue Pond.

III

AUTO ROADS WITHIN THE PARK

THE ROAD SYSTEM in Baxter Park is composed of one main gravel road with several short spurs. The road starts at the southern entrance of the Park, Togue Pond Gate, bears NW into the Nesowadnehunk Stream Valley, follows this northward to the west side of the Park at Nesowadnehunk Lake, then bears northeast and reaches the east side of the Park at Matagamon Gate near the outlet of Matagamon Lake. It is 43 mi. from Togue Pond Gate on the south to Matagamon Gate on the northeast.

Seven spur roads lead off the Perimeter Road: to Roaring Brook Campground on the east, Abol Pond, Daicey Pond Campground, Kidney Pond Camps, Nesowadnehunk Field, Nesowadnehunk Lake Gate, and to South Branch Pond Campground.

The Park roads are all gravel and **are not designed for rapid travel.** Visitors to the Park will be required to make a substantial adjustment in their driving to safely negotiate these roads. They are narrow and winding, with obstructed vision on curves. In many places when a car is met coming from the opposite direction, a visitor may be required to stop and pull over into a turnout to allow the other car to pass. **The speed limit on Park roads is 20 mph.**

The Perimeter Road is not designed or maintained as a scenic road for car travelers. For many miles the road travels through a tunnel of trees. There are, however, some viewpoints and numerous places of interest along the road, particularly if one parks the car and walks a short distance to scenic views.

Following is a description of the Perimeter Road with mileages in both directions of travel.

The Perimeter Road

Mileage North from Togue Pond Gate ↓		Mileage South from Mata- gamon Gate ↑
0.0	Togue Pond Gate House.	43.1
0.1	Junction with Roaring Brook Campground Road.	43.0
3.1	Junction with Abol Pond Road.	40.0
5.8	Pass Abol Campground	37.3
8.0	Junction with road leading 0.1 mi. to Katahdin Stream Campground.	35.1
8.2	Cross Katahdin Stream; junction with road to Katahdin Stream Campground.	34.9
8.7	Appalachian Trail leaves road to west.	34.4
10.7	Junction with road leading 1.4 mi. to Daicey Pond Campground.	32.4
10.9	Enter Foster Field Camping Area. Junction with road leading 1.4 mi. to Kidney Pond Camps.	32.2
14.0	Reach picnic area at site of old Slide Dam.	29.1
15.7	Pass Ledge Falls picnic area.	27.4
17.3	Junction with Nesowadnehunk Field Campground Road.	25.8
20.0	Nesowadnehunk Lake Gate	22.1

(cont.)

The Perimeter Road (cont.)

Mileage North from Togue Pond Gate ↓		Mileage South from Mata-gamon Gate ↑
29.3	Pass Burnt Mt. picnic area.	13.8
31.5	Pass Black Brook Farm site.	11.6
36.1	Reach The Crossing picnic area and junction with road to South Branch Pond Campground.	7.0
40.5	Reach Trout Brook Farm Campground.	2.6
43.1	Matagamon Gate House, 27 mi. west of Patten.	0.0

ROAD MILEAGES BETWEEN KEY POINTS WITHIN BAXTER PARK	Matagamon Gate	Trout Brook Campground	South Branch Pond Campground	Nesowadnehunk Lake Gate	Nesowadnehunk Campground	Kidney Pond Camps	Daicey Pond Campground	Foster Field	Katahdin Stream Campground	Abol Campground	Roaring Brook Campground
Togue Pond Gate	43	40	38	20	13	12	12	11	8	6	8
Roaring Brook Campground	51	48	46	28	25	20	20	19	16	14	
Abol Campground	37	34	32	14	11	7	7	5	2		
Katahdin Stream Campground	35	32	30	12	9	4	4	3			
Foster Field	32	29	27	9	6	1	1				
Daicey Pond Campground	34	31	29	11	8	3					
Kidney Pond Camps	34	31	29	11	8						
Nesowadnehunk Campground	26	23	21	3							
Nesowadnehunk Lake Gate	23	20	18								
South Branch Pond Campground	9	7									
Trout Brook Campground	3										

IV

CAMPING IN AND AROUND THE PARK

BAXTER PARK, being a wilderness park, has limited overnight camping capacity. Slightly more than one thousand
people per night can be accommodated. Private campgrounds
around the outside perimeter of the Park accommodate a lesser
number.

This limited capacity means that it is sometimes difficult to
obtain camping accommodations during the peak hiking season
from mid-July to mid-September.

The Park facilities are available on a reservation basis. This
requires registration and prepayment for these limited facilities
with the Reservations Clerk at Baxter Park Headquarters in Millinocket (207-723-5140) or 64 Balsam Drive, Millinocket, ME
04462. **Phone reservations are not accepted.**

Visitors who arrive at the Park in peak hiking periods without
reservations must take pot luck. Often the Park will be filled
and accommodations must be found elsewhere.

If the Park is at capacity, there is no prohibition on camping
outside the Park at one of the area private campgrounds and
then day-hiking in the Park.

**There are no facilities to accommodate self-contained or
sleep-in type camping vehicles in the Park.**

1. THE PARK'S CAMPGROUNDS

There are nine campgrounds within Baxter Park. Seven of these
are of the drive-in type. The other two are reached by back-

packing. Following is a description of each of the campgrounds and their facilities.

Abol Campground

Abol Campground was established in 1958 at the point where the Abol Trail leaves the Perimeter Road. It is a drive-in type campground with the following facilities:

   12 lean-tos (each 4 capacity)
    9 tent sites
    3 day-use tables and fireplaces.

The campground has two brooks passing near the lean-tos providing cold drinking water. A ranger is on duty at this campground.

Trails usually hiked from this campground are:

Abol Trail to Baxter Peak	3.8 mi.
Little Abol Falls Trail	0.8 mi.

A young Steve Clark (left) helping to build a lean-to.

All other trails in the SW Park area can be reached by short drives of 2–8 mi.

Katahdin Stream Campground

This drive-in campground is located along Katahdin Stream, off a short spur of the Perimeter Road. It is a beautiful spot with views of the Hunt Spur, Witherle Ravine, and the Owl. There is a small dam and pool in the campground's center. This area was formerly a gravel-washed, overgrown clearing. In 1934 the CCC (Civilian Conservation Corps, a depression-era public service organization) built six log lean-tos. Additions have been made from time to time to reach its present capacity. A ranger is on duty at this campground.

    12 lean-tos (3 3-person, 5 4-person, 4 5-person)
    10 tent sites
     1 bunkhouse (6 person capacity)
     9 picnic table sites

The Appalachian Trail passes through the campground and utilizes the Hunt Trail to the summit of Katahdin. Trails usually hiked from this campground are:

Hunt (Appalachian) Trail to Baxter Peak	5.2 mi.
Katahdin Stream Falls via A.T.	1.1 mi.
The Owl Trail	3.2 mi.
Grassy Pond Trail	1.5 mi.
Appalachian Trail to Daicey Pond	2.3 mi.

Other trails on the SW Park area can be reached by a short drive of 2–5 mi.

Daicey Pond Camps

Daicey Pond Camps were formerly on old-time sporting facility which was operated by the York family from the 1930's to the late 1960's. Like all sporting camps in Maine, it consisted of a main building containing a dining room and kitchen, a small recreation building (lodge), a number of guest cabins and support buildings such as owner's camp, guide's camp, and workshop. It is now run as a guest facility for Park visitors. The old dining room-kitchen building has been torn down, but the other buildings are intact. Reservations may be made for the guest cabins.

These log cabins are provided with bunks and mattresses, a stove, table, and chairs. Cooking must be done outside the cabins. They are beautifully situated on the NW shore of Daicey Pond with one of the best views in the Park of Katahdin. Firewood must be bought as is the case in most campgrounds. It is a good family campground because there are many easy hikes to surrounding ponds, streams, and waterfalls. Canoes may be rented to be used on the pond.

The capacities of the cabins are:

  4 2-bed cabins
  1 3-bed cabin
  6 4-bed cabins
  2 4-person lean-tos (for A.T. hikers)
  Cots for children are also available.

Daicey Pond is on the Appalachian Trail and is the registration point for A.T. hikers entering the Park from the south. A ranger is on duty here.

Trails usually hiked from this campground are:

A.T. south to Toll Dam, Little Niagara, and Big Niagara, all on Nesowadnehunk Stream	2.0 mi.
Grassy Pond Trail to K.S. Campground	1.5 mi.
Elbow & Tracy Ponds Trails (via A.T. north)	1.4 mi.
Sentinel Mountain Trail	3.9 mi.
Lily Pad Pond Trail	1.1 mi.
Kidney Pond Trail	1.0 mi.

The campground is located on a 1.4 mi. spur road which leaves the Perimeter Road near Foster Field. All other SW Park trails are easily reached by a short drive of 2–5 miles.

Kidney Pond Camps

Kidney Pond Camps is a private sporting camp on leased land within Baxter Park. See section on private campgrounds for descriptions of this facility.

Roaring Brook Campground

This campground is perhaps the most important (and the busiest) in the Park, since it is the access point for the two walk-in campgrounds, Russell Pond to the north and Chimney Pond to the west. It is also the key access point for all trails in the southeastern part of the Park. More day hikes can be taken from this point than from any other in the Park, including most points on Katahdin.

The campground, established in 1949–50, is located on Roaring Brook at the end of an eight-mile spur road which leaves the Perimeter Road at Togue Pond Gate. Sandy Stream Pond is close by, which is a popular spot because of frequent moose sightings.

All hikers bound for Chimney Pond, Russell Pond, or any of the interior parts of the Park to the north must leave their cars in the large parking lot at the campground. A ranger is on duty here.

Facilities are:

    12 lean-tos (3 2-person, 7 4-person, 2 6-person)
    10 tent sites (including 4 that are walk-in)
     1 bunkhouse (accom. 12)
     2 picnic tables

Trails which are hiked from this campground are:

Chimney Pond Trail	3.3 mi.
Helon Taylor Trail to Pamola Peak	3.2 mi.
Sandy Stream Pond Trail	1.3 mi.
South Turner Mt. Trail	2.0 mi.
Russell Pond Trail	7.1 mi.

All Katahdin trails including Dudley, Cathedral, Saddle, Knife Edge, Hamlin Ridge, and Blueberry Knoll trails can be reached from here.

Two miles to the south of Roaring Brook Campground is Avalanche Field, a group campsite situated on Avalanche Brook. A number of large groups can be accommodated at this site. Two lean-tos are also located here for group use. It is administered as a part of the Roaring Brook Campground.

An old unmarked tote-road to Katahdin Lake (3.3 mi.) starts from this site, but all of the SW Park trails are reached from Roaring Brook, a short distance away.

Chimney Pond Campground

By far the most spectacular campground in the Park and, perhaps, east of the Rockies, is at Chimney Pond. This is a shallow, glacially-formed pond surrounded on three sides by the two-thousand-foot wall and awe-inspiring granite cliffs of the Great Basin. The original cabin here was built in 1923 by the Maine Department of Inland Fisheries and Wildlife. For years, until his accidental death in 1942, this cabin was occupied by LeRoy Dudley, a legendary guide who for many years aided Katahdin climbers. There is also a bunkhouse which is insulated for winter use. **There is no tenting here** because of the accumulative adverse effect it would have on the very fragile mountain environment present at this altitude (2,914 ft.).

Because of years of firewood scavenging in the areas surrounding the campground, only limited quantities are occasionally available. Therefore, gas stoves are required at this site. A ranger is on duty here.

The facilities are:

9 lean-tos (4-person)

1 bunkhouse (accom. 12)

This campground provides the best and closest access to all east side Katahdin trails.

Hamlin Ridge Trail	1.5 mi.
North Basin Trail	0.9 mi.
Saddle Trail (to Baxter Peak)	2.2 mi.
Cathedral Trail (to Baxter Peak)	1.5 mi.
Dudley Trail	1.3 mi.
Knife Edge	1.1 mi.

The Northwest Basin and North Peaks trails may also be reached from here.

Chimney Pond is a walk-in campground, reached from Roaring Brook Campground via the Chimney Pond Trail (3.3 mi.)

The Davis Pond Lean-to in the Northwest Basin is administered from this campground.

Russell Pond Campground

This campground is located on a remote pond in the center of the Park miles from cars, roads, and the large numbers of people who tend to congregate around Katahdin. It is in an area about as wild as the Park has to offer and has many streams, ponds, and lakes nearby. Trails radiate outward in all directions to even more remote sections of the Park.

The campground was established in 1950 on the site of the sporting camps formerly operated by W. F. Tracy. The ranger station is one of the old camp buildings.

Moose are frequently seen in Russell Pond and the surrounding small ponds. Fishing is usually good in this area. Canoes may be rented for a small fee for use on these ponds.

The area is rich in history as nearby Wassataquoik Stream was the means by which timber was removed from this valley during several lumbering operations between 1880 and 1915. Many interesting remains of these operations are still to be seen in the valley.

The facilities here are:

    4 tent sites

    4 lean-tos (2 4-person, 1 6-person, 1 8-person)

    1 bunkhouse (accom. 12)

There are a number of remote wilderness campsites which are associated with Russell Pond. These are located at:

    Wassataquoik Stream on Tracy Horse Trail, 2 lean-tos (accom. 3 each)

    Wassataquoik Lake, a small cabin and tent site on an island.

    Little Wassataquoik Pond, 1 lean-to (accom. 3)

    Pogy Pond, 1 lean-to (accom. 3)

Interesting features reached from this campground are the Grand Falls of the Wassataquoik, a number of sites of old lumber camps or dams, Inscription Rock, the wild Northwest Basin, and crystal-clear Wassataquoik Lake.

Russell Pond is usually reached by the Russell Pond Trail (7.1 mi.) from Roaring Brook. It can also be reached from the west via the Wassataquoik Lake Trail (11.2 mi.) which starts on the Perimeter Road near Nesowadnehunk Lake, or from the north via the Pogy Notch Trail (9.6 mi.) starting at South Branch Pond Campground.

Other trails from this campground other than the three mentioned above are:

Tracy Horse Trail	3.9 mi.
Lookout Trail	0.9 mi.
Grand Falls Trail	2.1 mi.
North Peaks Trail	5.7 mi.
Northwest Basin Trail	8.4 mi.

Nesowadnehunk Field Campground

Nesowadnehunk Field Campground is located on the edge of an old lumber camp field, along the banks of Nesowadnehunk Stream in the west central section of the Park. It was established in 1953. It is a good base to climb the outstanding high peaked mountains which wall in both sides of the Nesowadnehunk Valley just south of the campground. A ranger is on duty.

The facilities located here are:

11 lean-tos (1 3-person, 10 4-person)
12 tent sites
 3 picnic sites
 2 group camping areas

There is only one trail originating from the campground, the Doubletop Trail (3.1 mi.) However, the following trails can be reached by a short drive of 2–5 miles:

Marston Trail to South and North Brother Mts.	3.8 mi.
Mt. Coe	2.8 mi.
O-J-I	2.9 mi.
Burnt Mt.	1.0 mi.
Wassataquoik Lake Trail	11.2 mi.

There are a number of scenic attractions close to the Perimeter Road in this area. Nesowadnehunk Lake is nearby which offers extensive canoeing, boating, swimming, and fishing. The Perimeter Road follows Nesowadnehunk Stream south from the campground. There are several outstanding vistas along the stream. One is at Ledge Falls, a huge smooth-rocked sluice 50 yards long. Another is the Slide Dam at the foot of a slide coming from South Brother. There are picnic facilities at both sites.

South Branch Pond Campground

After Chimney Pond Campground, the second most spectacular campground in the Park is South Branch Pond. Located on a gravel beach on the north shore of Lower South Branch Pond, it has good swimming, canoeing, and excellent climbing trails from the campground. The surrounding mountains are lower than the Katahdin complex to the south, so this fits more closely the requirements of family groups. There are numerous interesting geological highlights around the pond and on South Branch Stream. (See section on "Geology in the Park.")

The campground is located in the northern part of the Park on a 2 mile spur road from the Perimeter Road. It is most easily reached via the town of Patten and the Matagamon Gate. It was established in 1949 and there is a ranger on duty. Canoes may be rented for use on the pond.

The facilities are:

    12 lean-tos (4-person)
    21 tent sites
    1 bunkhouse (accom. 6)
    3 picnic sites

There are a wide variety of trails, ranging from easy hikes along ponds or streams to rugged scrambles over the Traveler Range. The Pogy Notch Trail leading south from the campground provides access to the wild interior of the Park around Russell Pond. The trails hiked from this campground are:

North Traveler Trail	2.7 mi.
Howe Brook Trail	2.0 mi.
South Branch Falls Trail	0.5 mi.
South Branch Mt. Trail	4.5 mi.
Center Ridge Trail	2.1 mi.
Ledges Trail	0.7 mi.
Middle Fowler Pond Trail to Barrell Ridge	3.0 mi.
Pogy Notch Trail (to Russell Pond)	9.6 mi.

There are two remote campsites reached from this campground. One is an attractively located 4-person lean-to at the southern end of Upper South Branch Pond. The other is further south on the Pogy Notch Trail on the NE shore of Pogy Pond. This is a small lean-to (accom. 3) located on a pine knoll overlooking the pond.

Trout Brook Farm Campground

Trout Brook Farm for many years was an important lumber camp and depot for the extensive lumber operations south and west of Matagamon Lake and up the Trout Brook Valley. At one time there were barns, blacksmith shops, storage houses, and camps for the lumber crews working the area. Foundations of several of these structures are still visible. The campground is located on the edge of the lumber camp field and is reached via the Perimeter Road, just east of the Matagamon Gate House.

It is the base for many hikes into the so-called Deadwater Mountains in the northern part of the Park. There are also a number of small trout ponds which are reached by trails originating along the Perimeter Road near here.

The extensive Matagamon-Webster wilderness north of the Perimeter Road is usually explored by using Trout Brook Farm as a base. It is a picturesque location, where wildlife literally abounds. It was established in the late 1960's as a means of providing access to the less frequented but outstanding wilderness located in the northern part of the Park.

The facilities here are only tent sites. There are 15 of them, plus a number of sites for large groups. Two trails originate from the campground. They are the new Trout Brook Mt. Trail, and the Freezeout Trail leading NW to the western end of Matagamon Lake and thence west to Webster Lake.

The trails within easy reach of this campground are:

Freezeout Trail	14.6 mi.
Trout Brook Mt. Trail	3.0 mi.
Webster Lake Trail	7.2 mi.
Fowler Brook Trail	1.3 mi.
Middle Fowler Pond Trail	1.7 mi.
Lower Fowler Pond Trail	2.7 mi.
Five Ponds Trail	3.9 mi.
Horse Mt. Trail	1.4 mi.
Burnt Mt. Trail	1.0 mi.

Since it is only seven miles from this campground to South Branch Campground via the Perimeter Road and a short spur road, all of the trails associated with that campground are also readily accessible from Trout Brook.

Moose are frequently seen in this area. Near Trout Brook is a short trail leading from the Perimeter Road to Littlefield Deadwater on Matagamon Lake. This is a good site for viewing moose.

There are a number of remote campsites associated with Trout Brook:

8 tent sites on the Fowler, Long, and Billfish ponds complex

5 tent sites along the Freezeout Trail, 2 of these on Matagamon Lake

1 lean-to (accom. 3) near the west end of Matagamon Lake

1 lean-to (accom. 3) on Webster Stream

3 tent sites on Webster Lake

1 tent site on Webster Lake Trail

3 tent sites on Matagamon Lake (must be reached by boat)

All of these are excellent wilderness campsites.

2. REMOTE CAMPSITES

For those who would prefer to get away from the congestion of the nine larger campgrounds, there is a limited number of remote campsites scattered around the Park. All require hikes to reach. They are either a simple tent site with a fireplace, or a lean-to. Reservations for these sites are made under the same procedure as sites in campgrounds. The lean-to at Davis Pond and the site at Wassataquoik Lake are exceptions. Reservations for these two sites are only made within seven days of their use.

Below is a list of these sites, their locations, and the campground with which they are associated. All lean-tos accommodate three people unless noted.

Remote Campsites		
Site	*Location*	*Associated with Campground*
Davis Pond Lean-to (accom. 6)	In NW Basin	Chimney Pond
Wassataquoik Lake Cabin	East end of Lake	Russell Pond
Little Wassataquoik Pond Lean-to	NW side of Pond	Russell Pond
Wassataquoik Lean-tos (2)	On stream at Tracy Horse Trail Crossing	Russell Pond
Pogy Pond Lean-to	NE side of Pond	South Branch
Upper So. Branch Pond Lean-to	South end of Pond	South Branch
Lower Fowler Tent Sites (2)	NE side of Pond	Trout Brook
Middle Fowler Tent Sites (2)	West end of Pond	Trout Brook
Long Pond Tent Sites (2)	E and N sides of Pond	Trout Brook

	Remote Campsites (cont.)	
Site	*Location*	*Associated with Campground*
Billfish Pond Tent Site	NW end of Pond	Trout Brook
Littlefield Pond Tent Site	N end of Pond	Trout Brook
Trout Brook Field Tent Sites (3)	1/2 mi. from campground	Trout Brook
Sawmill Tent Site	S shore Matagamon L.	Trout Brook
NW Cove Tent Site	SW shore Matagamon L.	Trout Brook
Little NE Branch Lean-to	West end Matagamon L.	Trout Brook
Webster Stream Lean-to	On Webster Stream	Trout Brook
Ice Wagon Tent Site	1 mi. E. of Webster L.	Trout Brook
Webster Lake Campsites (3)	On Webster Lake	Trout Brook
Eastern Tent Site	On Webster Lake Trail	Trout Brook
Matagamon Lake (3)	N shore Matagamon L.	Trout Brook

3. GROUP CAMPING AREAS

Large groups, such as scout groups, church youth groups, or camp groups have special needs which differ from other visitors to the Park. Because of greater space requirements and a group's natural exuberance, special areas have been set aside for their use.

It should be pointed out to all youth groups contemplating a visit to the Park that the dangers of a wilderness are different from other parks and present supervisory problems not encountered in other outdoor areas. Therefore, the Baxter Park Authority requires that all youth groups containing youngsters 16 years of age or less have adult (18 years or older) supervision in the ratio of 5 to 1. This may seem burdensome, but safety is much more of a factor in a wilderness.

Youth groups may use regular campgrounds when space is available, but group areas should be utilized to maintain the tranquility of wilderness campgrounds. The three areas follow.

Avalanche Field
This is located in the SE part of the Park and is a base for climbing all points on Katahdin. It can accommodate up to 50 people in four sites. It has two lean-tos and several fireplaces. It is located on the Roaring Brook Road, two mi. south of Roaring Brook Campground. Avalanche Brook passes through the campground. An old unmarked tote-road leading to Katahdin Lake (3.3 mi.) begins from this field.

Foster Field
This area is located on the western side of the Park two miles north of Katahdin Stream Campground and is administered by that campground. The Perimeter Road passes through the Field.

This campground provides a good base to climb all trails in the SE part of the Park, including the Hunt and Abol Trails up Katahdin. It also provides a good base for all the high peaks on the west side of the Park such as Doubletop, North Brother, and Mt. Coe. The trails to O-J-I leave this field, and the trailhead for the Doubletop Trail (south side) is about ½ mi. away. It has a capacity of 50 people. Nesowadnehunk Stream passes just west of the field providing good swimming in pools.

Nesowadnehunk Field
This area is also located in the western part of the Park, but further north than Foster Field. It is actually a part of the Nesowadnehunk Field Campground and has a capacity of 50 persons. Both Little Nesowadnehunk and the main Nesowadnehunk Stream pass through this field. There are swimming opportunities in stream pools and in Nesowadnehunk Lake, three mi. away.

This is a good base to use for climbing many of the high peaks along the Nesowadnehunk Valley such as Doubletop, South Brother, North Brother, Mt. Coe, and O-J-I. The Doubletop Trail (north end) starts about 1/2 mi. from the group site.

4. PICNIC SITES

The Park administration has located a number of picnic sites along the Park's road system to provide stopping places for visitors traveling from one part of the Park to another. These usually consist of picnic tables, often with a protective roof and a fireplace.

All of the drive-in campgrounds, with the exception of Daicey Pond, have picnic areas. In addition, there are picnic areas at the following sites.

At Rum Brook on the Roaring Brook Road.

At Abol Pond on the west end of that pond reached by a short side road from the Perimeter Road. This site also has a small but delightful sand beach for swimming.

At Foster Field on the Perimeter Road, at the southern end of the field.

At Slide Dam on the Perimeter Road, several miles north of Foster Field, on Nesowadnehunk Stream. The Marston Trail up North Brother starts at this point.

At Ledge Falls on the Perimeter Road, two miles south of Nesowadnehunk Field. This is a beautiful site with Nesowadnehunk Stream flowing over a series of smooth granite ledges.

At Burnt Mountain on the Perimeter Rkad, north of McCarty Field.

At Trout Brook Crossing on the Perimeter Road, at the point where the road crosses Trout Brook.

5. PRIVATE CAMPS AND CAMPGROUNDS

Around the outside perimeter and along the approach roads to Baxter Park are a number of privately operated camps and campgrounds. The distinction (at least in Maine) between these two entities is that camps have enclosed buildings such as a log cabin or a lodge, whereas a campground is for tenting and trailer use and in a few cases will include lean-tos.

Many people who have self-contained recreational vehicles, which cannot be used within Baxter Park, will find safe haven at these sites.

The camps often sell meals and frequently serve these in a high quality fashion. These camps usually consist of a group of cabins with a central dining hall and provide simple accommodations. Some charge extra for the use of canoes or boats. These camps tend to cater to people who like to hunt or fish, but an

Photographer George Hallowell took many of the photos in the Avery Collection, including this self-portrait.

increasing number of other outdoors people are using this type of accommodation.

Below is a list of camps and campgrounds. Many of the camps have telephones either in the Millinocket or Patten exchanges.

Private Camps

Only Kidney Pond Camps lies within the Park boundary. It is located on that pond at the center of a network of trails radiating to outlying trout ponds. Being located in the southwestern part of the Park, they offer excellent access to all mountain trails in that area such as The Sentinel, O-J-I, Doubletop, or North and South Brother.

As of the winter of 1987–88 the Baxter State Park Authority is exploring options for these camps. They may be converted to park use similar to nearby Daicy Pond Campground. As of the date of publication of the third printing of this book, no final decision as to the type of operation for Kidney Pond Camps has been made.

On the road from Millinocket to Baxter Park are located the following camps.

Millinocket Lake Camps, P.O., Millinocket, ME, 8 mi. north of Millinocket on a large lake.

Frost Pond Camps, P.O., Millinocket, ME

Katahdin Lake Camps, P.O., Millinocket, ME. Requires walking in 3 mi. or flying in from Millnocket Lake. Outstanding views of Katahdin, sand beach.

Prays Cottages, P.O., Millinocket, ME

Camp Wapiti, P.O., Millinocket, ME

Campgrounds

These are tent sites or places where recreational vehicles are accommodated. Some are quite attractively located and well managed, others have crowded sites and limited facilities.

On the road from Greenville to the Park is **Lily Bay State Park,** on the west shore of Moosehead Lake about ten mi. north of Greenville. It is run by the State and is an excellent facility, especially for those making long approach drives to Baxter and who have not reserved accommodations. It is rarely filled. There is swimming, boat launching, and well-laid-out campsites.

On the road from Millinocket are the following campgrounds.

Millinocket Lake Campground, eight mi. north of Millinocket.

Togue Pond Campground, located at the southern entrance to the Park. A good place to stay if the Park is full.

Abol Bridge Campground on the Greenville-Millinocket Road at that road's crossing of the West Branch of the Penobscot River, four mi. west of the Togue Pond Gate.

Pray's Wilderness Campground on the West Branch of the Penobscot.

Frost Pond Campground is located to the west of the Park and is reached from Ripogenus Dam on the Greenville-Millinocket Road.

Nesowadnehunk Lake Wilderness Campground is located at the south end of the lake, just off the Park property. It provides excellent access to the western and northern parts of the Park. It can only be reached from the west over G.N.P. private roads. The campground also has a small grocery store and gas pump.

On the road from Patten to the Matagamon Gate are the following.

Seboeis Stream Campsite is a Maine Forest Service campsite, open to the public, and is located where the road crosses this stream. Limited facilities.

Matagamon Wilderness Campground is located on the East Branch of the Penobscot River and is a good place to stay for access to the northern part of the Park. It is two mi. from the entrance gate. Matagamon Lake is 1/2 mi. from here. This is often the starting point for the East Branch canoe trip.

Shin Pond Village Camping at Shin Pond (P.O. Patten, ME).

WIND CHILL CHART

WIND IN MILES PER HOUR

	5	10	15	20	25	30	35	40	45	50
35	33	21	16	12	7	5	3	1	1	0
30	27	16	11	3	0	-2	-4	-4	-6	-7
25	21	9	1	-4	-7	-11	-13	-15	-17	-17
20	16	2	-6	-9	-15	-18	-20	-22	-24	-24
15	12	-2	-11	-17	-22	-26	-27	-29	-31	-31
10	7	-9	-18	-24	-29	-33	-35	-36	-38	-38
5	1	-15	-25	-32	-37	-41	-43	-45	-46	-47
0	-6	-22	-33	-40	-45	-49	-52	-54	-54	-56
-5	-11	-27	-40	-46	-52	-56	-60	-62	-63	-63
-10	-15	-31	-45	-52	-58	-63	-67	-69	-70	-70
-15	-20	-38	-51	-60	-67	-70	-72	-76	-78	-79
-20	-26	-45	-60	-68	-75	-78	-83	-87	-87	-88
-25	-31	-52	-65	-76	-83	-87	-90	-94	-94	-96
-30	-35	-58	-70	-81	-89	-94	-98	-101	-101	-103
-35	-41	-64	-78	-88	-96	-101	-105	-107	-108	-110
-40	-47	-70	-85	-96	-104	-109	-113	-116	-118	-120
-45	-54	-77	-90	-103	-112	-117	-123	-128	-128	-128

CURRENT TEMPERATURE

6. PRECAUTIONS FOR CLIMBERS

Many people visiting Baxter Park with the goal of ascending Katahdin underestimate the danger involved in climbing a major peak of this kind. The mountain has substantial trail mileage above tree line and at high (for the Eastern U.S.) elevations. This **exposure** is the main danger to take into account in climbing Katahdin. Other than the normal falls, which are a danger in climbing any mountain, the most serious accidents or near accidents have been associated with exposure. It may seem morbid to mention that a number of people have died on Katahdin, but hikers must constantly be aware that weather on Katahdin **can** be dangerous, even **FATAL.**

The Mountain should be regarded as subject to Arctic conditions and treated accordingly.

Analysis of mountain accidents shows that (*a*) hikers errantly proceeded into an exposed area during marginal weather conditions (high winds, precipitation, or both), or that (*b*) hikers were caught in exposed areas by sudden and unanticipated changes in weather conditions without proper protective clothing. Both of these situations must be carefully avoided in climbing above tree line. All climbers should be equipped with adequate clothing in the event of a change of weather conditions. Maps, compass, matches, flashlight, and emergency food should be carried. Some type of rain gear which can double as a windbreaker is essential. Hats and proper foot gear are important. Elsewhere in this guide is a wind chill chart which will show the rather startling effects wind can have on the loss of body heat. Study it carefully.

Careful preplanning of the hike can often prevent fatal mistakes. A reading of guide book descriptions and planning for bad weather descent routes will allow the hiker to make more intelligent, possibly critical, choices during the hike.

There are daily weather condition postings at all campgrounds. The Ranger's advice should be sought if in doubt.

The climbing of Katahdin is an all-day affair. Most routes involve a round trip of 8–12 miles and a net elevation gain of 4000 ft. Starts should be early, especially in late August and September when the shortened days end around six P.M. Eight o'clock or before is a good start. In July the main climb should be accomplished before the heat of mid-day.

Other than in wet seasons or after a heavy rain, it is generally desirable to carry a canteen. There are three major springs on the mountain. **Thoreau**, on the Hunt Trail, **Caribou** on the Northwest Basin Trail, and the **Saddle Spring** on the Saddle Trail. The latter is often unreliable in mid-summer to late fall.

Someone, preferably a Ranger, should know your itinerary for the day so that if an accident should occur your non-arrival back at camp or at your destination will be noted. This is a simple but often vital precaution. Most campgrounds will have a sign out sheet near the ranger cabin.

7. TECHNICAL CLIMBING IN THE PARK

The sheer faces of the Great Basin and other sites in the Park do offer excellent **technical rock climbing.** Before such climbing may take place several general **requirements must be met.**

All technical climbing must be preregistered and approved by the Baxter Park Authority. It must be proven that the climbing party has the technical experience and equipment to undertake such climbing. Adequate back-up protection must be arranged in case of accident (winter months only).

Parties contemplating technical climbing should write or call the Supervisor, Baxter Park Authority, Millinocket, ME.

8. WINTER USE OF THE PARK

The Park in recent years has seen a rise in the popularity of winter hiking and camping. The Park in winter is much more a true wilderness due to its remoteness. The roads are not plowed.

Up to 80 men would spend the winter in a camp like this one.

Therefore, long approach treks are required. Snow depths of four to seven feet on the level are common.

The bunkhouses at several of the campgrounds are often utilized as shelter on winter trips, but many parties now use modern winter tenting equipment during their stays.

All winter trips to the Park must be preregistered with the Park officials. They must determine the competency of each group as well as the adequacy of the party's equipment before granting a special use permit. Applications must be submitted to the Millinocket office of the Authority at least two weeks in advance.

Persons desiring to enter the Park on a day-use basis for cross-country skiing, snowshoeing, or similar activities need only register to use the Park.

V

GENERAL INFORMATION

1. THE PARK'S MOUNTAINS

There is a substantial concentration of mountains in the Park. They range from the massive, above-tree-line peaks that make up the main Katahdin Range to the rugged peaks which tower over the Nesowadnehunk Stream Valley, to the low rolling mountains in the northern parts of the Park that mark the northern end of the Appalachian Mountains.

Over half of these mountains, mostly the lower peaks in the northern half of the Park, do not have marked or maintained trails to their summits. These require "bushwhacks," a term used by climbers to describe a unique form of self-torture accomplished by crashing through trailless woods, swamps, and thickets where even rabbits wouldn't venture. Hikers are requested by Park authorities to preregister bushwhack trips with rangers before undertaking this type of hike.

There is some debate among climbers on what constitutes a mountain. Long arguments over hot campfires have resulted in consensus that a mountain is higher than its surrounding land; requires more physical effort to climb than walking on the level; is a grand place to be on sunny days, and not so good on rainy days.

Other than this, no firm agreement is forthcoming. Nonetheless, following is a list of mountains in the Park which are significant enough to have names. Some have more than one peak, but are dealt with as one mountain. There are 48, of which 21 are higher than 3,000 ft. Whether it has a trail or not is noted, as well as the Township and general location.

A Township is a unit of land area used in the unorganized lands in Maine. They are most often 6 miles square but are many times irregularly shaped. They are described by Township numbers on an east-west axis and Range numbers on a north-south axis (example, T5 R9, T5 R10, or T6 R10).

MOUNTAINS IN BAXTER PARK

Mt. or Peak	Elev.	Trail	Location
Baxter Peak	5,267 ft.	yes	T3 R9, So. Park
So. Peak	5,240	yes	T3 R9, So. Park
Pamola Peak	4,902	yes	T3 R9, So. Park
Chimney Peak	4,850 (app.)	yes	T3 R9, So. Park
Hamlin Peak	4,751	yes	T3 R9, So. Park
No. (Howe) Peak (2 Pks.)	4,734	yes	T3 R9, So. Park
No. Brother Mt.	4,183	yes	T4 R10, So. Park
So. Brother Mt.	3,930	yes	T3 R10, So. Park
Fort Mt.	3,861	no	T4 R10, So. Park
Mt. Coe	3,764	yes	T3 R10, So. Park
The Owl	3,736	yes	T3 R10, So. Park
Barren Mt. (3 Pks.)	3,681	no	T5 R9, So. Park
Traveler Mt.	3,541	no	T3 R10, No. Park
Doubletop Mt. (2 Pks.)	3,488	yes	T4 R10, Cntrl. Park
Mullen Mt.	3,450	no	T3 R10, So. Park
O-J-I	3,410 (app.)	yes	T3 R9, So. Park
Rum Mt.	3,361	no	T4 R9, So. Park
No. Turner Mt.	3,323	no	T4 R9, Cntrl. Park
The Cross Range (4 Pks.)	3,225	no	T4 R10, No. Park
No. Traveler Mt.	3,144	yes	T5 R9, No. Park

(cont.)

MOUNTAINS IN BAXTER PARK (cont.)

So. Turner Mt.	3,122	yes	T3 R9, So. Park
Wassataquoik Mt.	2,984	no	T4 R10, Cntrl. Park
Center Mt.	2,902	no	T4 R10, Cntrl. Park
No. Pogy Mt.	2,830	no	T5 R9, Cntrl. Park
Russell Mt.	2,801	no	T4 R9, Cntrl. Park
So. Pogy Mt.	2,705	no	T4 R9, Cntrl. Park
So. Traveler Mt.	2,677	no	T5 R9, Cntrl. Park
So. Branch Mt. (2 Pks.)	2,599	yes	T5 R9, No. Park
West Peak	2,485	no	T3 R10, So. Park
Strickland Mt.	2,390	no	T5 R10, Cntrl. Park
Bald Mt.	2,333	no	T5, R9, No. Park
Abol Mt.	2,306	no	T3 R9, So. Park
Lord Mt.	2,225	no	T5 R10, Cntrl. Park
Black Brook Mt. (2 Pks.)	2,223	no	T5 R9, No. Park
Big Peaked Mt.	2,130	no	T5 R9, No. Park
Barrell Ridge	2,067	yes	T5 R9, No. Park
Little Peaked Mt.	1,950	no	T5 R10, No. Park
Squirt Dam Mt.	1,931	no	T5 R9, No. Park
Sable Mt.	1,893	no	T5 R9, No. Park
Center Peak, Bullfish Mt.	1,880	no	T5 R10, No. Park
McCarty Mt.	1,870 (app.)	no	T3 R10, No. Park
Sentinel Mt.	1,837	yes	T5 R10, So. Park
Burnt Mt.	1,793	yes	T5 R10, No. Park
Morse Mt.	1,774	no	T6 R9, No. Park
Trout Brook Mt.	1,767	yes	T4 R9, No. Park
Tip Top Mt.	1,730	no	T4 R9, Cntrl. Park
Howe Peak	1,650	no	T5 R10, Cntrl. Park
Horse Mt.	1,589	yes	T6 R8, No. Park

2. KATAHDIN

KATAHDIN[1]
By Myron H. Avery

Katahdin, northern terminus of The Appalachian Trail, is one of its most outstanding features. Rising as an isolated, massive, gray granite monolith from the central Maine forest, broken only by the silver sheen of its countless lakes, Katahdin is indeed the monarch of an illimitable wilderness. It is a mountain preeminent — concededly it is without peer east of the Rocky Mountains! To the Indians it was known as "Kette-Adene" — the "greatest mountain" — and this mountain mass in every way responds to the tribute of the age-old name given it by the aboriginal dwellers in the fastness of the Maine forests.

From each cardinal direction, Katahdin's aspect is utterly different. It is not one but many mountains. From the south, seen over Togue Ponds on the Millinocket approach to the mountain, it is a huge, undulating rampart wall. From the east, over beautiful Katahdin Lake, it is the rim of a series of broken-open volcanic cones. From the north, it is merely the culminating peak of two parallel ranges which approach it from the level lands of the Penobscot East Branch Valley. From the west it is a long ridge, overtopping the outlying protecting barrier ranges.

"The distinctist mountain to be found on this side of the continent," wrote Theodore Winthrop of Katahdin in *Life in the Open Air*, that classic of the Maine woods. And apart from the mountain itself, the view from Katahdin furnishes all-sufficient answer to any query, Why climb Katahdin? "It is as if," one climber wrote, "a mirror had been broken and scattered over the mantle of the dark

---

1. Reprinted, with revisions from the illustrated booklet, *Mount Katahdin in Maine*, second edition, 1935, issued by the Maine Development Commission. (This publication is no longer available.)

green of the spruce and fir forest cover, for so do the myriad lakes heliograph to the summit. This pattern is broken only by the mountains and ridges, lying in every direction. One soon despairs of any attempt to count the number of lakes visible on a clear day."

The mountain itself may be aptly, if not elegantly, described as an enormous flat fishhook. The projecting point is the broad, rounded dome of Pamola (4,902 ft.) To the Indians, Pamola was the deity of the mountain. In awe of Pamola's wrath, the Indians never dared venture too near Katahdin. Those who accompanied Charles Turner, Jr., in 1804 told him how Pamola had destroyed a party of Indians who had previously ventured into the fastness of Katahdin, so that none then dared approach the mountain.

Enclosed in the bend of this hook, which extends at first south, then west and north, are three enormous basins — Great, North and Little North. These are split open to the east. The Great or South Basin, at an elevation of 2,910 ft., has on its floor two ponds — Chimney, about eight acres in extent, and a smaller hidden pond, known as Cleftrock Pool. From the floors of these Basins, sheer gray or pink granite walls rise abruptly over two thousand feet to the rim above. Here is a transported bit of the high Sierras or the Cascade Mountains of far west. With the rising sun or moon illuminating its walls, the Great Basin in its solitude creates an indelible impression of a strange, awesome and indescribable beauty. East of the Rocky Mountains, only in the Presidential Range in New Hampshire is found a mountain presenting such Alpine and glacial features as does Katahdin.

Encircling the Great Basin, for three-quarters of its circumference, is the famous Knife-Edge, a narrow wall of vertically-fractured granite. In many places one may stand astride of it; below, its precipitous slopes fall almost sheer for 1,500 feet. The Knife-Edge leads gradually upwards, past South Peak to Baxter Peak (originally named Monument Peak), just thirteen feet under a mile in height. Here is the summit of Katahdin. This, too, is on the rim encircling the Great Basin.

The broad summit of Katahdin, The Tableland, extending south and west for a mile and north for about three miles, is decidedly unexpected after the impression of a narrow mountain rim, created by the views from below. To the north from the summit—and forming the shank of the hook—The Tableland descends to its lowest point, The Saddle. It then rises to Hamlin Peak (4,751 ft.). North of Hamlin Peak is a long ridge containing the three bare Peaks North (Howe) (4,612 to 4,734 ft.). Then a long ridge, covered at first with a dense growth of scrub and then by a spruce and fir forest, extends north to Wassataquoik Stream.

A deep wide ravine divides the north end of Katahdin. On the east is the square bulk of Russell Mountain; to the west is Tip-Top, on the slope of which are the remains of an old sluice, originally used to drop logs into a pond formed by the splicing together of two streams in E.B. Draper's Wassataquoik lumber operations in 1910–14. High on the slope of Tip-Top is a rarely visited pond.

West of Katahdin is The Klondike, a great, elevated, forbidding spruce-flat, lying between Katahdin and the L-shaped Katahdinauguoh. The Klondike was long a land of mystery. Other than the famous Penobscot Indian Joe Francis, who hunted moose there and named the region because of its suggestion of the wilderness of the Canadian Klondike, few parties have traversed The Klondike.[2] No trails lead into it or through it. At its upper end, it is a

---

2. This was true in 1935. In the past 30 years, with increasing visitors to Katahdin, there has been quite an increase in trips into the Klondike. The number of such trips is not known, but probably there are several each year.

broad level expanse, enclosing several deadwaters on the Middle Branch of Wassataquoik Stream which rises here. Except by climbing over the surrounding ranges, the only approach to The Klondike is a tortuous way from the northeast along the stream where it has forced its way through the narrow, dark and gloomy defile between Fort Mountain and the Northwest Plateau.

On the west side of the mountain high above The Klondike are three other ravines, also of glacial origin. Perhaps the most interesting is the Northwest Basin (2,800 ft. app.) on the shelf of which are located five ponds. The outlet of Lake Cowles, the largest pond, cascades from the shelf to the Northwest Basin Brook below. A waterfall, dropping from the slope of the mountain, is the inlet of Davis Pond. On the upper reaches of the Northwest Basin Brook is a long line of waterfalls.

Klondike Pond (3,435 ft.), on the south side of the Northwest Plateau, is a narrow body of water, a third of a mile in length, in a wild and picturesque ravine located high above The Klondike.

Witherle Ravine is an enormous chasm, near The Gateway, descending to Katahdin Stream under the shadow of the cliffs on The Owl.

What has been said here is a mere enumeration of the outstanding features of Katahdin. The casual climber, who thinks he has seen all after he reaches Baxter Peak, knows little of the wonders of Katahdin. It is a mountain not for a one day's trip but for many days and to which the traveler will return again and again with increasing pleasure and enthusiasm.

The master architect, which so skillfully sculptured this most fascinatingly shaped mountain, was the glacier which stood down over New England eons ago. The mountain's original form, shape or height is a matter of the vaguest conjecture. The continental glacier has planed off the top, leaving the massive, flat Tableland rising toward the south. Then later, local glaciers carved out the three cirques or basins which are so prominent on the east side of the mountain. Deeper and deeper they scoured and cut back into the Great Basin until only the narrow rim of the Knife-edge remained to connect the massive, rounded peak of Pamola with the rest of the mountain. In front of the Basins the debris, moved outward by the glacier in the form of moraines, has resulted in a chain of five ponds, strung across the mouths of the three Basins.

On the west side of the mountain the two most interesting features are also glacial relicts — Klondike Pond, located in a narrow, deep ravine dug out half-way down the mountain's slope, and the Northwest Basin. The sheer walls of these cirques and the freshness of the glacial work tell even the most uninitiated in the study of the mysteries of the earth that these glaciers have only recently departed. It has been estimated that the last local glacier disappeared from Katahdin's slopes between ten and fifteen thousand years ago. The traveler along the crest will take keen interest in searching for glacial erratics, which are quite different from the granite of the mountain and were transported from the north and deposited by the glacier when it overrode the summit of Katahdin.

As the present shape of the mountain was determined in the glacial period, so was its vegetation. The flora of Katahdin is arctic. It is an island, a relict of the vegetation which followed the retreating glacier back north. The plants on the summit are those now found in Greenland and northern Labrador. Some of the scientific names of the commonest plants tell significantly of their present habitat — thus, *Arenaria groenlandica* and *Diapensia laponica*. A vast museum for the geologist, the botanist, and the biologist, Katahdin looms like an open book for even the most untutored in the natural sciences.

Katahdin is indeed a mountain preeminent.

3. OTHER MOUNTAINS IN THE PARK

From the south, Katahdin is a solitary mountain. From other directions, it is merely the lofty culmination of a long line of satellite peaks which lead to it from the north. These peaks, magnificent in themselves, suffer only from the misfortune of lying close under the dominating shadow of Katahdin. Were Katahdin not here, these outlying mountains alone would provide outstanding experiences for the visitor. Lower and less rugged, these peaks were known to the Indians as the "Katahdinauguoh." Moses Greenleaf, Maine's first mapmaker, wrote of this range in 1820.

> On the north-west and north (of Katahdin), a cluster, termed by the Indians Katahdinauguoh, extends to a considerable distance, and is connected with or separated only by small and narrow ravines and valleys from a succession of mountains and ridges which form the Aroostook and Allagash range, and the whole collectively may be appropriately denominated the Katahdin range.

There is a fascinating region directly north of Katahdin — Russell, Fort, Wassataquoik, Mullen, and Pogy mountains and that gem of mountain lakes, Wassataquoik. Further southwest are North and South Brother, the culminating summits of the Katahdinauguoh, rising over 4,000 ft. in height. Together with Mt. Coe, these peaks form the beautiful, symmetrical line of summits known as The Brothers.

The rock pinnacles on the dense scrub-covered cone of The Owl, the long ridge of Barren, O-J-I with its name-plate washed out by the slides following the September 1932 storm, and the inverted V-shaped slide on Mt. Coe, afford strenuous but most rewarding trips from either Katahdin Stream, Abol or Daicey Pond Campgrounds, or from the Perimeter Road. Two trails, utilizing the slide, reach the crest of O-J-I, affording views of The Klondike.

Nestled between Wassataquoik Mountain and the broad expanse of South Pogy Mountain, with its ruins of its lumbering past, is Wassataquoik Lake. Narrow and walled-in by sheer cliffs, it is a setting perhaps unequalled in the State. Beyond Pogy Mountain is a cross-range (east and west) of Burnt, Squirt Dam, Black Brook, Black Cat, and South Branch mountains. Burnt Mountain affords a fine outlook over the entire region.

Across the flat Pogy Notch looms another parallel range. From the old firetower on Matagamon or Horse Mountain, rising abruptly from the lake of that name, there extends south and west a series of bare rhyolite cones — The Deadwater Mountains — which in 1846 had indelibly impressed Thoreau. The peaks of this group, all easily climbed, are Trout Brook Mountain, the three peaks of Billfish Mountain, and Bald Mountain. On the summit of Bald Mountain is a small growth of *pinus banksiana*, first reported there by the State Geologist Survey in 1861.

South lies The Traveler. Its descriptive name was applied by voyageurs on the Penobscot East Branch; the mountain seemed to travel with them. For many years it was thought to be the second highest mountain in the state. Only recently has The Traveler been forced to yield this distinction to a peak in western Maine. Prior to the building of the Grand Lake Road, The Traveler was seldom climbed. To the west, five spurs extend from its long, bare ridge. Two side-ridges wall in the two South Branch Ponds, whose spectacular beauty has few rivals in the State. To the east of The Traveler is a less-frequently visited region.

The Traveler and The Deadwater Mountains are most easily reached from the Perimeter Road and South Branch Ponds Campground.

Across from Katahdin, to the east, is the broad expanse of Turner Mountain, with its North, South, and East peaks. On the east side is the misnamed Twin Ponds in a glacial cirque, hemmed in by sheer cliffs. From South Turner, easily reached from Roaring Brook Campground, there is a magnificent view of Katahdin and its basins. Twin Ponds is accessible from the camps at Katahdin Lake.

From Daicey and Kidney ponds on the west side of Katahdin, Doubletop's cone — perhaps Maine's most perfectly shaped mountain — offers a full but rewarding day's trip. Trails also lead from Daicey and Kidney ponds to low-lying Sentinel Mountain with a splendid, grandstand view of the Katahdin Range from the west.

4. PONDS AND STREAMS IN THE PARK

Maine is known for its thousands of lakes and ponds, and Baxter Park has its share of them.

There are sixty-four (count 'em) named ponds or lakes (or groups of them). Most of these are small ponds of less than 100 acres. The largest water bodies are Matagamon and Webster lakes to the north, and Nesowadnehunk Lake in the west. Ponds or lakes in the Park vary considerably in depth, from Davis Pond at 5 ft. to Matagamon Lake at 95 ft.

A few of the larger lakes, such as Nesowadnehunk or Matagamon, have dams to control water flow, but most are damless and are at natural water levels. Some ponds were dammed in the past to build water heads for log driving, such as Wassataquoik Lake or Basin Ponds.

Many of the ponds are isolated and seldom visited, except by occasional fishermen. They are characterized by rocky shores and clear waters and are exquisitely beautiful. They are natural centers for wildlife. Moose claim them for their own during the late summer.

Some are located in flat country and are usually surrounded by a spruce-fir shoreline. Others are located between steep mountains with sheer cliffs dropping into the pond. Upper South Branch Pond is an excellent example of this type. Sand beaches are at a premium in the Park. Togue and Abol ponds have several, as does Matagamon Lake. The water level on Matagamon Lake varies considerably as the Bangor Hydroelectric Company owns a large dam at its outlet and draws down the lake when water is needed by power-generating dams further down the Penobscot. This variance in water level detracts from the otherwise attractive features of Matagamon.

There are a number of high-mountain ponds which are called **tarns**. Notable are Chimney, Basin, Klondike, Davis, Traveler, and Lake Cowles. These are located at high elevations, Klondike Pond being the highest at about 3,400 ft.

They are not usually deep ponds, contrary to popular belief, although Lake Cowles is a deep, cold, 52 ft. and the Basin Ponds are a respectable 30 ft. But Davis Pond is a chest-deep 5 ft. and Chimney Pond is only 15 ft. None of these ponds (other than Traveler Pond) are able to maintain a fish population because of the depth of ice formation in winter and the lack of food.

WATER BODIES IN BAXTER PARK

Water Body Name	Township Location	Area (acres)	Max Depth (feet)
Abol Pond	T2 R9	70	34
Basin Ponds	T3 R9	35	30
Bell Pond	T4 R9	-	-
Billfish Pond	T6 R9	70	84
Blunder Pond	T6 R10	-	-
Celia Pond	T3 R10	8	17
Center Pond	T4 R10	-	-
Chimney Pond	T3 R9	6	15
Cranberry Pond	T2 R9	-	-
Daicey Pond	T3 R10	38	26
Davis Pond	T3 R9	3	5
Deep Pond	T4 R9	8	20
Deer Pond	T3 R10	-	-
Depot Pond	T3 R9	-	-
Draper Pond (two ponds with this name)	T3 R10	10	12

(cont.)

WATER BODIES IN BAXTER PARK (cont.)

Water Body Name	Township Location	Area (acres)	Max Depth (feet)
Draper Pond	T4 R9	-	-
Dwelly Pond	T5 R10	19	4
Elbow Pond	T3 R10	13	5
Foss & Knowlton Pond	T3 R10	41	21
Frost Pond	T6 R9	37	32
Grand Lake Matagamon	T6 R8	4165	95
Grassy Pond	T3 R10	-	-
High Pond	T6 R9	17	15
Hudson Pond	T6 R10	-	-
Jackson Pond	T3 R10	23	33
Kidney Pond	T3 R10	96	33
Klondike Pond	T3 R9	8	8
Lake Cowles	T3 R9	10	52
Lily Pad Pond	T3 R10	20	15
Littlefield Pond	T6 R9	-	-
Little Fowler Pond	T5 R9	-	-
Little Rocky Pond	T3 R10	16	22
Little Wassataquoik Lake	T4 R10	10	10
Long Pond (two with this name)	T4 R9	-	-
Long Pond	T6 R9	70	33
Lost Pond	T3 R10	-	-
Lower Fowler Pond	T6 R9	64	15
Lower South Branch Pond	T5 R9	93	60
Mahar Pond	T5 R9	-	-
Martin Ponds	T3 R9	-	-
Middle Fowler Pond	T5 R9	45	27
Mink Pond	T2 R9	-	-
Mountain Catcher Pond	T6 R8	90	16
Nesowadnehunk Lake	T4 R10	1394	46
Rat Pond	T2 R9	-	-
Rocky Pond (two with this name)	T2 R9	10	8
Rocky Pond	T3 R10	29	22

WATER BODIES IN BAXTER PARK (cont.)

Water Body Name	Township Location	Area (acres)	Max Depth (feet)
Round Pond (two with this name)	T2 R9	8	19
Round Pond	T6 R9	6	31
Rum Pond	T2 R9	-	-
Russell Pond	T4 R9	20	6
Sandy Stream Pond	T3 R9	17	4
Six Ponds	T4 R9	61	17
Tea Pond	T2 R9	-	-
Tracy Pond	T3 R10	12	4
Traveler Pond	T5 R9	-	-
Twin Ponds	T4 R9	-	-
Upper South Branch Pond	T5 R9	84	76
Upper Togue Pond	T2 R9	294	34
Wassataquoik Lake	T4 R9	178	79
Webster Lake	T6 R10	531	44
Weed Pond	T4 R9	-	-
Whidden Ponds	T3 R9	-	-
Windy Pitch Ponds	T3 R10	-	-

The only large river in the Park is a small section of the East Branch of the Penobscot River and a large tributary of that river, Webster Stream. These are located in the northern part of the Park. Webster Stream is the main inlet to Matagamon Lake. The East Branch resumes its river course after escaping through the Grand Lake Dam near the Matagamon Gate entrance of the Park.

There are three other major streams in the Park. Nesowadne-hunk Stream has its source from that lake, and flows south draining the west side of the Park. Trout Brook drains the north central part of the Park. Wassataquoik Stream drains the central and east sides of the Park. Nesowadnehunk and Wassataquoik streams are large mountain streams with an ability to rise rapidly in heavy rains. They have beautiful falls, ledges, sluices, and at a few locations, dark, quiet pools. They are in every sense classic mountain streams.

Sandy Stream is a smaller watercourse which drains the southwest part of the Park around Roaring Brook.

In high water these streams should be treated with extreme caution as they develop powerful currents that can and have swept people to a watery death.

All these streams were the means by which lumber was harvested and removed from this area dating back to the 1830's. They are tied inexorably to the lumbering lore of the region. Names of features along these streams were labeled by lumbermen, such as Toll Dam, Slide Dam, New City, Mammoth Dam, Windy Pitch, and Indian Pitch.

There are many, many other streams or brooks in the Park. Some of the better known are Abol Stream, Katahdin Stream, Roaring Brook, and South Branch Stream.

5. FISHING IN THE PARK

Because of the great number of ponds, lakes, and streams in the Park, fishing is a major recreational activity. Native brook trout is the main species caught, although some Blueback trout have been landed in Wassataquoik Lake and a sprinkling of Sunapee trout in South Branch Ponds. Matagamon and Webster are the only lakes with the right conditions to maintain any sizable numbers of landlock salmon.

Luckily, the Park's waterways have not been seriously infested with yellow perch, smelt, or other non-game species.

But fishing enthusiasts who are not familiar with the highs and lows of the manic-depressive native trout should be forewarned that the Park's waters are hardly the proverbial "fisherman's paradise" where trout are ravenous, hook-eating, finned friends that strike at the drop of a dry fly or the plop of a worm.

Like most trout fishing, when they bite they go crazy and when they don't, no fly will entice them. So timing is critical.

The time of the year also has a great bearing on success as the peak of the season is in June. In later summer, trout usually seek out colder water in which to congregate.

All waters in the Park are subject to laws and regulations of the Inland Fisheries and Wildlife Dept. Fishermen must have a State of Maine fishing license. This applies to both resident and non-resident fishermen. A copy of the current Fish and Wildlife regulations should be examined to determine bag limits and restrictions on use of lures or bait.

As previously mentioned, there are no fish in Chimney, Basin, Klondike. Davis ponds, or Lake Cowles so don't waste your time unless you are fishing for frustration.

The unquestioned, most fabulous fishing spot in the whole Park is _____ Pond. Good fishing!

6. WILDLIFE

The most common large "game" animals of Baxter State Park are the moose, black bear, and white-tailed deer.

Moose in particular are plentiful in Baxter State Park and are commonly seen during the summer months at Sandy Stream Pond near the Roaring Brook Campground, Russell Pond, Turner Deadwater, the outlet of Nesowadnehunk Lake, Dwelly Pond, Tracy Pond, Stump Pond, Littlefield Deadwater, and McCarty Field. Moose prefer ponds surrounded by marsh during the summer months because of the plentiful food supply and relief from insects. During September and October they are commonly seen along the Perimeter Road, Nesowadnehunk Field, McCarty Field, Trout Brook Farm, Russell Pond, and Turner Deadwater. **Caution should be exercised with cow moose** accompanied by calves in the spring, and bull moose during the mating season (mid-September to mid-October).

Black bear are also common throughout Baxter Park. They are observed lunching in raspberry patches during August and on beech ridges in October. **Caution should be observed with all**

bears. Do not attempt to feed them as they can be **aggressive** and **dangerous**.

White-tailed deer are also numerous in Baxter State Park. They are commonly observed along the Perimeter Road and throughout the Park. Daicey Pond and South Branch Pond campgrounds sometimes have deer that can be hand fed. Neso-wadnehunk Field, McCarty Field, Foster Field, and Trout Brook Farm have occasional appearances of deer.

Beaver, muskrat, mink, otter, and raccoon are plentiful along the marshes, streams, and lakes of Baxter Park. Nesowadnehunk Stream, South Branch, and Trout Brook have vibrant beaver colonies close to the Perimeter Road. Scavenging raccoons are active in all the Park campgrounds, particularly at night. They are the best known of woodland bandits.

Bobcat, lynx, red fox, fisher, marten, weasel, snowshoe hare, porcupine, red squirrel, and chipmunks are common in all

Don't ever approach bears in the Park, even babies like these.

wooded areas of the Park. The red squirrel is also a noisy tenant in all campgrounds.

In recent years a new denison of the north woods country has filtered into Baxter Park. The eastern coyote, locally known as a coy dog, has made his presence known. Coyotes are wary hunters and are rarely seen. Their dog-like footprints, frequently encountered, mark their wide-ranging travels.

7. BIRDS

The Park is literally a bird watcher's paradise. Because of the wide variety of habitats, such as alpine tundra, virgin forest, and harvested forest, a diversity in species is possible. Also, the relatively low interference from human activities allows certain species to flourish which could not do so in other areas of the Northeast.

Below is a list of the species which have been observed and identified at one time or another in the Park.

Mockingbird	Bald Eagle
Ruby-throated Hummingbird	Common Eider
American Bittern	Purple Finch
Brewer's Blackbird	Flicker
Red-winged Blackbird	Crested Flycatcher
Bobolink	Least Flycatcher
Snow Bunting	Canada Goose (migrating)
Catbird	Snow Goose (migrating)
Boreal Chickadee	American Golden-eye
Black-capped Chickadee	Barrows Golden-eye
Cowbird	American Goldfinch
Brown Creeper	Goshawk
Red Crossbill	Grackle
White-winged Crossbill	Rose-breasted Grosbeak
Crow	Evening Grosbeak
Black-billed Cuckoo	Pine Grosbeak
Mourning Dove	Ruffed Grouse
Rock Dove (Pigeon)	Spruce Grouse
Black Duck	Glaucous Gull

(cont.)

BIRDS (cont.)

Herring Gull
Broad-winged Hawk
Red-shouldered Hawk
Sharp-shinned Hawk
Kestrel (Sparrow Hawk)
Great Blue Heron
Blue Jay
Canada Jay(Moose Bird)
Slate-colored Junco
Killdeer
Eastern Kingbird
Golden-crowned Kinglet
Ruby-crowned Kinglet
Belted Kingfisher
Common Loon
Mallard
American Merganser
Red-breasted Nuthatch
White-breasted Nuthatch
Baltimore Oriole
Osprey
Owls
Phoebe
Raven
Redpoll
Robin
Spotted Sandpiper
Solitary Sandpiper
Yellow-bellied Sapsucker
Northern Shrike
Pine Siskin
Snipe
Chipping Sparrow
Field Sparrow
Fox Sparrow
Song Sparrow
Tree Sparrow
White-crowned Sparrow
White-throated Sparrow

Barn Swallow
Tree Swallow
Starling
Scarlet Tanager
Terns
Brown Thrasher
Hermit Thrush
Wood Thrush
Towhee
Veery
Red-eyed Vireo
Backburnian Warbler
Bay-breasted Warbler
Blackpoll Warbler
Black-and-white Warbler
Canada Warbler
Cape May Warbler
Connecticut Warbler
Chestnut-sided Warbler
Magnolia Warbler
Mourning Warbler
Myrtle Warbler
Nashville Warbler
Parula Warbler
Pine Warbler
Redstart
Tennessee Warbler
Wilson's Warbler
Worm-eating Warbler
Yellow-throated Warbler
Cedar Waxwing
Woodcock
Whip-poor-will
Downy Woodpecker
Hairy Woodpecker
Pileated Woodpecker
Three-toed Woodpecker
House Wren
Winter Wren

8. WILDFLOWERS

Baxter Park contains a wide diversity of wildflowers normally found in and around the northern spruce-fir and hardwood forests.

In addition, flowers, shrubs, and other plants found only in the arctic tundra are present in the alpine zone on Katahdin. These plants are found infrequently east of the Mississippi, mostly in the White Mountain alpine zones.

Below is a list of wild flowering plants found mainly in the lower elevations.

Trailing Arbutus (Mayflower)
Twinflower
Bloodroot
Violets (purple, yellow, white and blue)
Bunchberry
Checkerberry
Partridgeberry
Indian Pipe
Jack-in-the-pulpit
Skunk Cabbage
Trillium (Painted Purple)
Wind Flower
Columbine
Buttercup
Wild Rose
Blueberry
Blackberry
Raspberry
Strawberry
Chokeberry
Shadbush
Mountain Ash
Clover (pink, yellow, and white)
Rhodora (Azalea family)
Fireweed
Cranberry (low and highbush)

Lady's Slipper
Goldthread
Dutchman's Breeches
Spring Beauty
Ground Nut
Joe-pye Weed
White Summer Daisy
Queen Anne's Lace
Fall Blue Aster
Goldenrod
Cardinal Flower
White Aster
Common Bladder Campion
Wild Onion
Cotton Grass
Yellow Cowslip
Yellow Adder's Tongue
Marsh Marigold
Pitcher Plant
Meadow Rue
Wild Oats
Pearly Everlasting
Indian Paintbrush
Bluet
Mustard
Honeysuckle
Sweetpea Vetch
Lupine
Forget-me-not

(cont.)

WILDFLOWERS (cont.)

Thistle	Solomon Seal
Troutweed	Butter-and-eggs
Pickerelweed	Dandelion
Wood Lily	Orchid Plant
Lily-of-the-valley	Flag Iris

Mountain flowers of the Heath Family (*Ericaceae*) are found above timberline on Katahdin and in lower bog areas.

Mass Plant	Sheep Laurel
Labrador Tea	Pale Laurel
Bog Rosemary	Velvet-leaf Blueberry
Leather-leaf	Low Sweet Blueberry
Rhodora	Mountain Heath
Lapland Rosebay	Mountain Cranberry
Alpine Azalea	Wren's-egg Cranberry
Creeping Snowberry	Bog Bilberry
Alpine Bearberry	Dwarf Bilberry

Reference

Mountain Flowers of New England, 1964, Appalachian Mountain Club, 5 Joy St., Boston, MA (Illustrated).

9. GEOLOGY OF THE PARK

Baxter Park is a geologist's heaven because of the wide variety of phenomena which can be observed there. Even for non-geology types, the physical features of the Park can be curious, interesting, and even awe inspiring.

What person can walk into Chimney Pond Campground and not look up in wonder at the towering walls of the Great Basin? How did they come to be? On the Tableland, how did all those acres of same-sized granite rocks come to be there? What causes

Dry Pond to become dry in summer? How did the long gravel ridge north of Togue Pond come to be? Was it a dumping ground for a construction site? What causes ten-foot-round holes in solid rock in the stream bed of Howe Brook that make private, but cold, bathtubs? What are all those strange seashell-like rocks on the lake shore, a hundred miles from the sea? Why is some of the Katahdin granite grey in color on the lower slopes but pink in the upper elevations? What force caused those long scratches on the rocks?

All these questions are answered by understanding the geology of the Park. There are several good books on the subject. The best for the beginner is the illustrated *Geology of Baxter State Park and Mt. Katahdin* by Dabney W. Caldwell (available through the Baxter Park Headquarters). Enough information to tantalize you is given here.

There are two main types of *bedrock* in the Park: Katahdin granite, both the grey type, and the beautiful pink granite found at higher elevations; and in the northern part of the Park, Traveler rhyolite. The latter is of volcanic origin and is much more fine-grained than granite. It is mostly dark grey in color.

There are also other types of rock called *sedimentary rocks* which were formed by compressing mud or sand into shale or sandstone.

Fossils from ancient seas which covered this area are usually found in these types of rocks, particularly the shale. The best location to find shale rock is around the South Branch Ponds, but it is found to a lesser degree throughout the Park.

It should be noted here that removal of fossils is not permitted, except by permission of the B.P.A. for scientific purposes.

Some of the most interesting physical features of the Park have their origins in the age of glaciers. As most people will remember from their school days, thick (often a mile deep) sheets of solid ice covered this part of North America.

There are two types of glaciers: the covering-all *continental glaciers*, and valley or *local glaciers*. Continental glaciers are so powerful they tend to flatten everything in their path. The ice which covers Greenland is a good example of this type of glacier. Valley glaciers are much smaller and are contained within a given valley's walls. Glaciers in Switzerland and Alaska are good examples of these.

At the point where the ice of a glacier ends, a build-up of rock and gravel often occurs. This is called a *moraine*. Blueberry Knoll in the North Basin is a good example of this.

The Great Basin is an excellent example of a *glacial cirque*, which is a glacial, bowl-shaped valley with steep walls. U-shaped, glacially-formed valleys are distinguished from a V-shaped valley caused by water erosion. The U-shaped types are characterized by steep valley walls and broad valley bottoms. The Northwest Basin is a well-developed example. Most of the large valleys in the Park, whether they have a head (three sides) or are open at both ends fall into this category.

Narrow ridges such as the Knife Edge or Hamlin Ridge are called *arêtes*. This is caused by two local glaciers at work on either side of the ridge. The glaciers tend to bite into the walls causing them to become steeper and narrower.

Glaciers, besides ripping and tearing the rock over which they are passing, also *carry* and *deposit* this debris to various locations. A moraine is a good example of this action. Another is glacial *till*, a mix of clay, sand, gravel, and boulders. If these are cemented together by the clay, the resulting stone is called *conglomerate*. Huge rocks that are found out in the middle of the forest which did not fall from a nearby cliff were usually left by glaciers as well. They are called *erratics*.

An *esker* is an easily recognized glacial deposit because of its long, ridge-like shape (some being several miles long) and because of its rise in height from surrounding low land. They are composed of sand and gravel and make good roadbeds or trail paths. They are locally called "horsebacks." They are formed by running water building up these deposits in tunnels under the glacier. The esker that the Perimeter Road follows west from Togue Pond Gate for several miles is the best example. There is another one on a southeast-northwest axis north of Kidney and

Tracy ponds. A third, well-developed esker runs between High and Long Ponds on an east-west axis near Trout Brook Farm.

Many of the small, circular ponds in the Park are called *kettles* or *kettleholes*. These were caused by the melting of huge ice blocks (remaining after the main ice sheets had disappeared) with deposits building up around them. Russell Pond or Rat Pond are good examples.

On Howe Brook, under the shadow of the Travelers, are interesting features not caused by glaciers. In the brook are large cylinders worn in the grey rhyolite rock of the stream bed. These are known as *potholes* and are scoured out by the circular force of the stream over a long period of time. They provide rather unusual swimming.

Near the mouth of Howe Brook as it empties into Lower South Branch Pond is a huge, well developed *delta*. It forms a division between the two Branch ponds which were, in the distant past, one. This is easily seen from topographic maps.

There are many other interesting geologic features in the Park which may be examined by the person who is more interested in detail about this fascinating subject.

VI

HISTORY OF THE PARK

THERE IS so much written about Katahdin and the surrounding land that an entire library stack would have to be constructed to accommodate all the literature. Myron Avery, who compiled an annotated bibliography of Katahdin, said, "The surprising extent of the Katahdin literature is perhaps the best expression of the universal appreciation of this mountain, described by Theodore Winthrop as 'the best mountain in the wildest wild to be had on this side of the continent.' "

The history given here is, then, a condensation from a number of sources to provide the visitor to the Park with some background and flavor of the human events which have occurred in and around the Park.

1. THE INDIAN PERIOD

Back in the mists of time, the Indians were the first humans to travel around the Katahdin country. Most of the tribes lived close to the coast but ranged through the river valleys on hunting trips and visits to tribes living in the St. Lawrence Valley to the north. Although there were no permanent villages near the Katahdin country, it was well known and frequently visited by the more recent tribes of the Abenaki nation. There were several villages along the lower and middle Penobscot River.

Indians were not builders of lasting monuments. They were mainly simple hunters and fishermen with marginal farming to supplement their diets. Their lives were not easy, and many times they hovered close to the subsistence level.

Their proud culture is carried forth today mainly by two tribes, the Penobscots from Old Town, and the Passamaquoddys from eastern Maine.

Their place-names and folk legends about the area have been recorded and are now a part of written history.

2. INDIAN LEGENDS CONCERNING KATAHDIN

To many American Indian tribes a mountain was a home of some nature-deity. The Indian pronouncement on this subject was "Every mountain got Injin in it." The mountains were thought to be hollow and were the homes of ancestors, a deity of the trouble-making type, or friendly, even benevolent spirits.

Katahdin, being the tallest and most awe-inspiring mountain in the area, would be a logical choice for the best or worst of Indian spirits around; and so it was.

Actually, there were no less than three deities who were supposed to have their abode in or around Katahdin. Like most religions, there was an all-powerful, somewhat benevolent being, and its opposite number—a fierce, evil and dangerous thing. There was a third spirit, rather neutral in character.

White men have lumped all these spirits together and have fashioned one Indian god they find most interesting and romantic who most closely resembles their concept of a nature deity; the evil one.

The evil one was the Storm-bird present in many Indian cultures, and was similar to the Maliseet (Coastal Indians) *Culloo*. It was described as being a bird-like creature with a horrible beak, claws, and a "head as large as four horses." This being was the bringer of storms and trouble, and would smite down anyone who ventured too close to his mountain. White men have given this being the name of *Pamola* (from the Indian *Bumole*)

Paloma advises Maine Guide Leroy Dudley, a painting by Maurice "Jake" Day of Damariscotta, Maine.

and have elevated him to be *the* deity of Katahdin.

Maurice "Jake" Day of Damariscotta, Maine, has painted an interesting caricature of Pamola and pictures him to be more friendly, although still a zoologist's nightmare.

The neutral spirit was called *Wuchowen*, the spirit of the night wind, who was mostly a form made up of wings and created forest breezes by flapping its wings.

The third and most powerful of the triumvirate was the *Spirit of Katahdin*, a humanoid with "stony eyebrows and cheekbones" (a dead ringer for the Old Man of the Mountains of N.H.). There are a number of tales that describe this spirit's relationship with the Indians. The best was a story told many years ago to Fannie H. Eckstorm, noted Maine Indian historian, by Clara Neptune, an old Indian woman. Even in her halting English and with the problems of translation from one culture to another, it is still a vivid, interesting account of how the Abenakis related to their deities. It is reprinted here in its entirety.

A Story As Told By Clara Neptune

"Ev'ry mountain got Injin in it. Katahdin, he man; mountain once was man." She went on to tell about a girl who used to live at Old Town, a beautiful girl and a great belle. "Name? Don't know it her name. No, not chief's daughter — just girl."

All the younger men courted her. "Used be anybody want girl, used take waubub (wampum) her folks. Young men all bring it bunches beads her folk; but dis girl don't want it anybody 't all. Good many fellows want her, couldn't get her."

"One time dancin' 'mong rocks, singin', singin'

'Ef he was man, Katahdin,
I would marry um;
I wouldn' marry no man dis world.' "

Each time the old lady varied the little song. "Got pretty

tune" she said, "used sing it that song myself." Once she gave it in Indian, and the translation is her own.

"Mothgehbeh Kathdinosis
(Ef he was Katahdin.)
Chewl medeh dahabah
(He wanted to marry me.)
"Nisweeoowaynewah"
(I would marry him.)

"Den came Katahdin. Somebady's he's standin' near his back, he seize um, carry um off." She was taken to Katahdin's home inside the mountain, for the mountain is all hollow inside. "Had it good wiguam-camp inside, big tent; boughs, everything. Dat ooman he dan' want nothin; victuals."

There she lived and in time was born little Kathdinosis, with the stony eyebrows. But Katahdin was away much of the time and the young mother longed to see her own father and mother and to show them her baby.

"Katahdin he told um, 'You want gone see you folks, you can gone see um father, mother. You take um baby.' "

"Den he carry his wife one day. 'You go see father, mother. Only little boy, don' make him low-arrow. When he see anythin' he p'int. Don't you let him anythin; danger — no low-arrow; no knife.' "

But the old man is so pleased with his grandson that he wants to amuse the child. "Dis ol' man when he see his daughter, dat leetle boy he got rock here — eyebrow, he set down outdoors, make um low-arrow his grandson. First thing he kill his grand-fadder. 'Fore dat he only p'int at bird, at deer, moose — kill um. Used be when he see bird flyin' he p'int at birds (laying one fore-finger over the other, crooked like a bow) p'int with finger like bow 'n arrow, and birds come down. Now kill grandpa.

"Den dat night he came get un Katahdin.

"Dat's what make um Inuuns down dere (in Katahdin). Mus' be good many of 'em dere now. Joe Francis his camp Debsco-neag, he can hear it gun, fiddle, hear um play bowl on moun-tain, livin' in Katahdin."

And she bent forward, intent as if listening to hear the magic flutes that you can hear at Joe Francis' camp on Debsconeag.

3. INDIAN PLACE NAMES AROUND KATAHDIN

Around Katahdin there is a rich legacy of Indian names for rivers, lakes, and mountains. These are intermixed with traditional English names such as Turner Mt., Russell Pond, or Trout Brook. At one time there were many more Indian place names, but as the English culture was superimposed over that of the Abenaki's the Indian names were forgotten or replaced. Thus, in the northern part of the Park, Namadunkehunk becomes Webster Stream.

Indians seldom named things after themselves. In their culture humans were not the centerpiece of existence. Like many hunting-fishing societies, they viewed themselves as subordinate to nature. So Indian names were almost always descriptive of the natural world around them such as "place of many fish" or "pond near the high mountain."

The name Katahdin itself is a good example, meaning "greatest mountain." This is why Katahdin in its correct form should never be preceded by Mt. or Mount. It would then become "mount greatest mountain." Katahdin, by the way, has had in the past various spellings such as Katadin, Ktaadn, Ktaahden, Ktahdin, or Taddn.

Below is a list of Indian place names around the Katahdin region which may be of interest to the visitor to this part of Maine.

ABOL "bare, devoid of trees" probably referred to the huge slide that adopts this name.

ABALAJACKOMEGUS "bald country, bare, no trees."

ALLAGASH "bark cabin" or birch-bark shelter.

AMBAJACK-MOCHOMAS (Falls) "slantwise of the regular route."

AMBAJEJUS (Lake) "two currents, one on either side of an island."

APMOOJENE-GAMOOK (Indian name for Chamberlain Lake), "lake crosswise" of the usually traveled route.

CHESUNCOOK "at the place of the principal outlet."

DEBSCONEAG "ponds at the high place" or "ponds at the head of the waters."

KATAHDIN "greatest mountain."

KINEO "sharp peak."

KLONDIKE "hammer water," referring to driving stakes into a watercourse so as to make a salmon trap.

KOKADJO "kettle mountain."

LUNKSOOS "a catamount" or a wildcat.

MATAGAMOOK (Matagamon Lake) "old exhausted lake," fished out, grown up with weeds.

MATTAWAMKEAG "at the mouth of a gravel bar." The Indians named the branch to a river by some easily recognized natural feature near its mouth.

MILLINOCKET "dotted with many islands and coves," refers to Millinocket Lake which fits this description.

MOLUNKUS "deep valley stream" or "ravine stream."

NAMADUNKEHUNK (Webster Stream) "straight-up-the-hill-stream."

NERLUMSKEECHTICOOK name given to the Deadwater Mountains north of Katahdin.

NESOWADNEHUNK (Stream) "swift stream between the mountains," or "swift stream in a mountain ravine."

PEMADUMCOOK (Lake) "extended sand bar place."

PENOBSCOT (River) "the rocky part" or "at the descending rock," which referred to a part of the river near Old Town.

POCKWOCKAMUS "little muddy pond."

RIPPOGENUS (Pond) "small rocks, gravel."

WASSATAQUOICK (Lake) "a clear shining lake."

WASSATAGWEWICH (the East Branch of the Penobscot) "at the bright sparkling stream."

References on Indian Place Names and Legends

Eckstorm, Fannie H., *Indian Place Names of the Penobscot Valley and the Maine Coast*, University Press, Orono, ME, 1941.

Eckstorm, Fannie H., *The Katahdin Legends*, Appalachia, Vol. 16, No. 1, December, 1924, P. 39.

Giles, John, *Memoirs of Odd Adventures*, Spiller & Gates, 1869, at Cincinnati.

Greenleaf, Moses, *Indian Place Names*, Privately printed, 1903.

Velromill, Rev. Eugene, *The Abnakis and Their History*, New York, James B. Kirner, 1866, P. 62.

4. EXPLORATION AND EARLY CLIMBS

Not all white men who came to the Katahdin area in the 1800's were looking for ways to turn a dollar. Many were explorers, adventurers, hunters, fishermen, and later, those who liked to enjoy the total outdoor experience in this area. Below is a chronological list of notable expeditions to the Katahdin area.

1764   A partial ascent by Joseph Chadwick, a surveyor.

1804   Ascent by Charles Turner, Jr. and a party of surveyors from Massachusetts. These are the first white men known to have reached the summit.

1819   Second ascent by British surveyors from the Maine Boundary Commission, led by Colin Campbell.

1820   A survey party from the Maine Boundary Commission.

1825   Monument Line surveyors, Joseph C. Norris, Sr. & Jr.

1836   First scientific excursion to Katahdin by Professor Jacob W. Bailey, et al.

1837   Ascent of Charles T. Jackson, State Geologist, during the first geological survey of Maine.

1845   Ascent by Rev. Edward Everett Hale and W. F. Channing.

1846   Ascent by Henry D. Thoreau.

1847   Rev. Marcus R. Keep (Keep Ridge is named after this man) made his first visit to Katahdin and ascended the mountain as far as Pamola. In 1848 he explored the Great Basin.

1856   Expedition of Theodore Winthrop and F. E. Church.

1877   Ascent of Frederick E. Church and party of artists.

1880–1901   George Witherle's excursion and climbs of the mountains in the Katahdin region.

1887   First Appalachian Mountain Club camp at Katahdin.

1892–1902   Various botanical expeditions by Briggs, Harvey, Fernald, and Cowles.

1916   Appalachian Mountain Club camp at Chimney Pond.

1921–1923   Exploration of the Klondike and Mayo Pond.

1920   The Percival P. Baxter excursion before he was Governor of Maine.

1923   Appalachian Mountain Club camp at Chimney Pond.

1925   The Governor Ralph O. Brewster party.

1925   Appalachian Mountain Club camp at Kidney Pond.

1930   First Baxter acquisition of land to become part of the Park.

1931   First transfer of land to the State and creation of Baxter Park.

1938   Completion of the Appalachian Trail across Maine to Katahdin.

1939   The Appalachian Trail Conference holds its 8th annual meeting at York's Twin Pine Camps on Daicey Pond.

1940–1962   Numerous acquisitions of land by Baxter complete the Park at over 200,000 acres.

1969   Percival P. Baxter dies.

1975   Over 8,000 people climbed Baxter Peak.

5. ROUTES OF THE EARLY EXPLORERS

As one might expect, in the early 1800's the hard part of climbing Katahdin was getting to it. Between the settlements along the coast and Katahdin lay a long upstream river canoe trip along the Penobscot with its many portages and few inhabitants. Most explorers approached the mountain via the West Branch. Once they arrived at the prominent point of land at the confluence of Abol Stream and the West Branch, the obvious route was seen. Abol Slide was the first route up the mountain, avoiding the sometimes almost impenetrable scrub near the tree line. This route was used by many of the early explorers including Turner in 1804, Jackson in 1837, and Thoreau in 1846.

Then the scene shifted. Lumber tote roads were opened on the east side of the mountain. This was coupled with the establishment of stagecoach lines north of Bangor to Mattawamkeag and Stacyville. This made it possible to take the stage from Bangor north, then use the tote roads north from Mattawamkeag or west from Stacyville avoiding the long, tedious, river approach. Thus from the 1840's to almost 1920, the bulk of climbers visiting Katahdin came from the east. In 1869 the European and North American Railroad crept north from Bangor to reach Mattawamkeag. And in 1894 the Bangor and Aroostook was built north from Bangor, crossing the East Branch of the Penobscot at Grindstone and passing on to Stacyville, thus continuing the access from the east.

The first trails up the mountain were usually a combination of lumber tote roads as far as possible, then crude paths, sometimes only axe blazes on trees, from there to the tree line of Katahdin.

The first of these trails was punched through from Katahdin Lake to the foot of the "East Slide" (the old St. John's Slide below Pamola Peak) by the Rev. Marcus R. Keep. Later he modified this to follow the long open ridge leading up to Pamola (named the Keep Path). This was done on several visits starting in 1846. The present Helon Taylor Trail follows much of this route. By 1874 lumbering operations had obliterated the below-tree line portions of it.

In 1874 two young entrepreneurs named Lang and Jones, who wanted to tap the increasing "sporting trade" to the mountain, opened a set of camps on the south shore of Katahdin

Lake. To provide a path for their patrons, they opened a rough trail to Sandy Stream, then up its branch, Roaring Brook, to Basin Ponds. Then it was an easy scramble to the tree line on Pamola, Hamlin Ridge, or ahead into the Great Basin. This was called the Lang and Jones Trail.

1887 saw the establishment of an Appalachian Mountain Club camp at the north end of Katahdin Lake. This group cut a new trail along the south flank of South Turner Mt., north of Sandy Stream Pond, and thence to Basin Ponds.

The intensive lumbering operations in the Wassataquoik offered new approach routes on tote roads from this direction. From a lumber camp (the McLeod Camp on the Upper South Branch of the Wassataquoik) the Rogers Trail led south near the mouth of the North Basin to Basin Ponds. A second trail from this camp, the McLeod Trail, ascended a long ridge directly to the tree line on the North Peaks. These were established around 1894 and were obliterated by the Great Wassataquoik fire of 1903 (as were most of the trails in this area).

Another trail associated with the Wassataquoik lumbering operations was the opening of the Tracy and Love Trail in 1884. The route of the present North Peaks Trail follows this old trail almost identically. This route was popular through 1924 but gradually fell into disuse as the Tracy Sporting Camp on Russell Pond declined in usage. It was re-cut in 1927 by a nephew of Tracy.

As the lumbering operations along the Wassataquoik and the east side of the mountain diminished and finally ended in 1914, the scene again shifted to the west. During the early 1900's, and particularly 1920–1930, a series of "sporting camps" were established on that side of the mountain. The two most prominent were at Daicey and Kidney ponds.

In 1890 Irving Hunt opened a trail on The Spur which now bears his name. This was materially improved by the CCC in 1934.

In addition the old tote road north of Millinocket was vastly improved so that travelers could take a train to Millinocket, then

Dynamiting a log jam.

Winching a "boom" of logs across the water.

use buckboard and later cars to approach the west side quite easily, compared to the old eastern approaches. About this same time The Grand Lake Road from Patten was opened to Trout Brook Farm, thus providing access from the north.

With the arrival of the 1930's, the present road approaches were established. The improvement of this system into the present Perimeter Road is the main factor leading to the construction, maintenance, and use of the present trail system in the Park.

From the 1930's to the late 1960's the Appalachian Mountain Club spent considerable effort opening and maintaining trails, both on the mountain and from the east.

1933 through 1938 saw the completion of the Appalachian Trail across Maine, terminating at Baxter Peak. In a sense, the completion of the A.T. to Katahdin marks the threshold in passing from the old exploration-expedition era to the modern backpacking-hiking era.

6. THE LUMBERING ERA

Contrary to popular belief, most of the land within Baxter Park has seen lumbering activities at one time or another from approximately 1830 to 1965. Some areas were harvested several times.

Timber was removed from this country by sending it down watercourses until the advent of the truck and the ability to construct elaborate haul roads (mainly after 1945).

The life of a lumberman was unbelievably hard. It was common for men to become old at forty. Long, often wet cold days, the roughest of lodging, and plain food was the rule. Thoreau, in his book *In The Maine Woods*, wrote the following description of their life.

It was easy to see that driving logs must be an exciting as well as dangerous business. All winter long the logger goes

An old-style campfire near the mountain.

A rare photo of the inside of a logging camp.

on piling up the trees which he has trimmed and hauled in some dry ravine at the head of a stream, and then in the spring he stands on the banks and whistles for Rain and Thaw, ready to wring the perspiration out of his shirt to swell the tide, till suddenly, with a whoop and halloo from him, shutting his eyes, as if to bid farewell to the existing state of things, a fair proportion of his winter's work goes scrambling down the country, followed by his faithful dogs, Thaw and Rain and Freshet and Wind, the whole pack in full cry, toward the Orono Mills. . .

He (the log driver) must be able to navigate a log as if it were a canoe, and be as indifferent to cold and wet as a muskrat. He uses a few efficient tools, — a lever commonly of rock maple, six or seven feet long, with a stout spike in it strongly ferruled on, and a long spike-pole, with a screw at the end of the spike to make it hold. The boys along shore learn to walk on floating logs as city boys on sidewalks. Sometimes the logs are thrown up on rocks in such positions as to be irrecoverable but by another freshet as high, or they jam together at rapids and falls, and accumulate in vast piles, which the driver must start at the risk of his life. Such is the lumber business, which depends on many accidents, as the early freezing of the rivers, that the teams may get up in season, a sufficient freshet in the spring, to fetch the logs down, and many others.

There were five watercourses large enough to utilize for driving timber within what is now the Park.

The first was Nesowadnehunk Stream, which was used to remove timber in most of the southwestern and western parts of the Park area to a point north of Nesowadnehunk Lake. This area was cut relatively early. Over a period of a hundred years an elaborate system of tote roads, dams, and camps was established. The Nesowadnehunk Tote Road, which the Perimeter Road utilizes from Abol Pond north to Nesowadnehunk Lake, and the remains of the old Toll Dam on Nesowadnehunk Stream near Daicey Pond are examples of these lumbering facilities.

The second watercourse was Sandy Stream. This allowed the removal of timber from the southeastern part of the Park. The area around Togue Ponds, Roaring Brook, Basin Ponds, and Sandy Stream Pond was harvested by the use of this stream. The Reed operation in 1874 was the first large-scale operation to use this stream, although smaller operations had used it before this time.

There were two large dams on this stream, plus a number of smaller ones. One was located near the site of the present Sandy Stream Dam. A second dam was located near where the present Katahdin Lake Tote-Road crosses Sandy Stream. This was called Hersey Dam. Remains of this dam are visible today.

Signs of this operation can be found on Sandy Stream Pond in that the pond has two outlets. The easternmost is the natural one. The western one was blown open to provide a shortcut for getting the wood into Roaring Brook with less trouble. There are other signs of this operation for the sharp-eyed hiker.

In later years, around 1920–30, the Great Northern Paper Company conducted commercial operations in this area and opened a tote road from Roaring Brook to Togue Pond. The present Roaring Brook Road follows the course of the older road. A branch of this road continued to Basin Ponds.

The Katahdin Lake area was cut and driven eastward down Katahdin Brook into the third watercourse, Wassataquoik Stream, and thence into the East Branch of the Penobscot. This was, in a sense, the classic operation in the Katahdin area. In the central part of the Park, roughly around Russell Pond, is a huge bowl that contained very valuable timber. But Wassataquoik Stream was wild and rocky, surrounded by very difficult terrain. There were four major operations to get the wood out. From 1883 to 1891 the Tracy & Love operation opened the area and started the removal. From 1891 to 1901 the Ayer and Rogers operation took over the job. Next the Katahdin Pulp & Paper Co., from 1901 to 1905, removed timber from the area. Last and certainly the largest was the Draper operation from 1910 to 1914. This marked the end of lumbering operations in the central area of the Park.

The remains of many structures are still visible. There were two dams on the Lower Wassataquoik outside the present Park. The Daicey Dam was located about a mile below the junction of Katahdin Brook and the Wassataquoik. The Robar Dam was located five mi. upstream at the junction of Twin Ponds Brook and the Wassataquoik.

The first lumber camp site within what is now the Park was a large lumber camp known as the Old City. This was located at the fork of Pogy Brook and the Wassataquoik. Old fields in the process of being reclaimed by the forest still mark this site.

The so-called Great Wassataquoik Fire of 1903 wiped this site clean. This was a huge, very intense fire, undoubtedly aggravated by prior lumbering excesses. This fire roared down through Pogy Notch which acted like a chimney flue, then fanned out in the central bowl around Russell Pond. It was so intense it even burned down through the humus. The area burned covered over 132 sq. mi.

Fires had swept the Wassataquoik before. In 1884 a smaller fire burned 22,000 acres in four days. A later fire also swept Pogy Mt. on May 28, 1915, just after the completion of the Draper operation.

The effects of these fires can still be seen in the areas north and east of Russell Pond. The trees here are spaced widely and at this late date, seventy years later, the accumulating new soil is just beginning to support larger trees.

Above the Old City site, and just above the Grand Falls of the Wassataquoik, was the Mammoth Dam. A mile above this in the stream bed is a huge rock called Inscription Rock. Here in 1883 some member of the Tracy & Love operation chiselled the name and date of the operation.

At a point near the present Tracy Horse Trail crossing of Wassataquoik Stream is the site of the South Branch Dam. An old lumber camp called the Bell Camps was located on the south shore at this point.

Just south of Russell Pond and along Turner Brook is a series of beautiful fields which are in the process of joining the forest. The old Wassataquoik Tote Road passes through the clearings, and the present Tracy Horse Trail follows the road. This was the site of the New City Camps. They were quite extensive, including a church, blacksmith shop, school, and many individual camps. They are all gone now, but depressions in the ground mark their locations. Old implements are strewn about these fields.

Above this point, which was the key camp in the later lumber operations, there were a number of structures. There were dams on the outlets of Wassataquoik Lake and Turner Deadwater, on Mullen Brook, and on the Middle Branch of the Wassataquoik, plus a number of smaller dams.

There was also a large sluice from South Pogy Mt. to the west end of Wassataquoik Lake. This was a large structure requiring a trestle-like support.

Outlying camps dotted the valley. The most notable ones, other than the previously mentioned New City site, were at Russell Pond and at Annis Brook. The latter location still has many implements lying about on the forest floor.

The fourth watercourse used for logging operations was Trout Brook. This allowed lumbermen to harvest timber in a huge area south and west of Matagamon Lake. The logs were driven into Matagamon Lake and then down the East Branch of the Penobscot.

The key facility in this area was Trout Brook Farm. The site was first cleared in 1837 for use in lumber operations. It was extensive and at its height contained many buildings and camps. The buildings were destroyed by fire three times. Foundations are still easily seen in the old fields.

The main way to reach Webster, Chamberlain, and Eagle lakes, and the huge area around them which could be harvested, was up the East Branch, through Trout Brook Farm, and thence NW to Webster and Telos Lakes. So the Farm was the main stopping place after ascending the East Branch.

Many companies ran this operation. The last was the Eastern Corporation which discontinued its activities in the early 1950's.

There were several small dams on Trout Brook. Black Brook Farm was an outlying camp operation further up the brook.

The fifth and last of the watercourses used to remove lumber from the area was Webster Stream and Webster Lake. This, in a sense, is a continuation of the East Branch of the Penobscot. The most notable structure on this course lies just west of the Park boundary. This is the famous Telos Cut.

Originally the waters of Telos, Chamberlain, Churchill, and Eagle lakes flowed north down the Allagash, into the St. John, and thence into Canada. Therefore lumbermen from Bangor could not harvest this area. Fortunately, by cutting a small canal between Telos Lake and a nearby ravine, then raising the water level in Chamberlain and Telos lakes by building a dam near its northern end, the watercourse could be reversed to flow south into Webster Lake, down Webster Stream and the East Branch of the Penobscot to Bangor. This was done in 1841 and opened a huge new area to harvest, all passing through the northern part of what is now the Park.

This cut can be seen (along with a dam at the east end of Telos Lake) by a short trip from Webster Lake. The Freezeout Trail now follows Webster Stream and provides access to this interesting area.

The present dam at the outlet of Matagamon Lake, and its predecessor, were important links in both the Trout Brook and Webster Stream operations. They lifted the level of the original rather shallow lake, making driving much easier and providing a head of water to drive the East Branch below the dam.

The logging era in the Park was extensive and provides the visitor who is willing to look closely with interesting relics of this era.

It will take many years for the Park to regain a forest growth similar to that which existed prior to the 1880's. The only major timber stands that escaped the lumbermen's axes and saws and the accompanying fires that swept the area were at the head of Howe Brook near the Traveler, and the entire Klondike Bowl. The latter was just too difficult to get out. There are additional small pockets on the high slopes.

References

The Appalachian Trail in Maine, Katahdin Section, 1969 Published by Maine Appalachian Trail Club.

Avery, Myron H., *An Annotated Bibliography of Katahdin*, Appalachian Trail Conference, 1950.

Avery, Myron H., *The Keep Path and its Successors*.

"The History of Katahdin from the East and North," *Appalachia* (A.M.C.), Vol. 17, No. 2, Dec. 1928.

Baxter, Percival P., "Mt. Katahdin State Park," an address at the annual meeting of the Maine Sportsman's Fish & Game Association, Augusta, 1921.

Eckstorm, Fannie H., "Thoreau and Ktaadin," *The Congregationalist*, August 1866.

Hempstead, Alfred G., *The Penobscot Boom and the Development of the West Branch of the Penobscot River for Log Driving, 1825–1931*, Printed Privately, 1975.

"The Sandy Stream and Mt. Katahdin," *Northern*, Vol. 3, No. 2, May 1923.

Thoreau, Henry David, "In The Maine Woods," *Atlantic Monthly*, Vol. 102, No. 2, August 1908.

Witherle, George H., "Excursions North of Katahdin," *Appalachia*, Vol. 3, No. 3, Dec. 1883.

VII
PARK TRAILS

THERE ARE 170 mi. of foot trails in the Park. For the visitor to see what the Park is all about, to savor the natural wonders and wilderness that so many seek, the trails are the best paths.

The Park's trails are not extensive compared to the White Mountains or other mountainous areas with elaborate trail systems. The bulk of the trails in Baxter Park are concentrated in the southern region around Katahdin. Over 100 of its 170 mi. are located in that area.

The trails might be classified into three categories according to their past development: those established by fishermen or area sporting camps as access trails to reach remote ponds; those which follow old lumber roads, sometimes called tote roads, which were generally established from the 1880's through the 1930's when the area was heavily cut; those established by hikers interested in access to the mountains, particularly Katahdin.

Each type of trail has its own character and each offers a very different type of hiking experience. The trails originally developed as fishing access trails usually involve a pleasant walk through dense woods terminating on the shore of a beautiful wilderness pond. The trails utilizing old tote roads usually follow mountain stream valleys with many pools, falls, and deadwaters. There are still many signs and relics of the lumbering era to be seen by the sharp-eyed hiker. The mountain hiking trails head for the hills and, of course, involve considerable exertion to attain the heights. Much of the climbing is above tree line, particularly on Katahdin.

All three offer quite a different aspect of the Park and all should be sampled to discover its wonders.

The Park's trails are well maintained as the Park officials have spent considerable effort in recent years to upgrade and improve the trail system. Emphasis has been on constructing erosion control devices to minimize damage to heavily-used trails. These require considerable effort to install but good results are already observable by the hiker.

The marking system used by the Park is a standard 2" x 6" paint blaze on rocks or trees. These are usually blue in color, although the Appalachian Trail uses white blazing.

Above tree line, cairns (rock piles of varying heights) are used. These are particularly effective on the flat expanses of the Tableland on Katahdin.

Because of the tendency of hikers to wander and widen trails above tree line (in some case trails are 40–50 ft. wide) steps are being taken to reconstruct trails, particularly on the Tableland. Here "trail hardening" techniques are being used to construct a stable, erosion-free path that the hiker will choose to follow.

Hikers are urged to stay on the trail in these fragile areas. Growth of small plants is so slow at these altitudes that even a slight amount of foot traffic can cause great damage.

Most hiking in the Park is done as day hiking rather than backpacking. This is true because of the proximity of the campgrounds to the main mountains. Katahdin is ringed by four of the Park's nine campgrounds, concentrating over half of the camping capacity within a day's hike of the main peaks of Katahdin.

There are only two campgrounds, having a combined capacity of less than 150 people, which are reached by backpacking. These are Chimney Pond in the Great Basin, and Russell Pond in the central part of the Park.

There is also a limited number of small remote campsites located in the central and northern part of the Park. Five of these are close to Russell Pond.

The predominance of day hiking in the Park should be noted

by those preparing to visit it. Backpacking equipment is not needed to hike in the bulk of the Park. But there are outstanding backpacking trips available, mainly north of Katahdin.

The description of the Park's trails is in four groups according to their geographical location. They are Southwest Park Trails, Southeast Park Trails, Central Park Trails, and Northern Park Trails.

The bulk of trails on Katahdin can be found in the two southern sections.

Trail descriptions are handled several different ways. A trail to a specific point, such as a mountain summit or a remote pond, will be described in detail from the trail head to the trail's end. Then a summary of the reverse mileage will be given back to the starting point.

Trails with starting points at both ends of the trail, such as the trail between Roaring Brook and Russell Pond campgrounds, will be handled differently. These will have detailed descriptions in both directions.

A third type of trail description is on a short trail, usually one mile or less. Only a general description will be given of these.

Times estimated in this guide are only rough approximations with no time allowed for stops.

SOUTHEAST PARK TRAILS

The trail system in the Southeast part of the Park is not extensive, consisting of about 28 mi., but is the most highly used in the Park. The reason for this is the trail system's proximity to the most spectacular feature of the Park, the Great Basin and the main peaks of Katahdin.

This huge, glacial, horseshoe-shaped cirque is ringed on three sides by a 2000-foot wall of granite cliffs. It has no equal east of the Mississippi. Connecting the easternmost peak of the cirque, Pamola Peak, with South and Baxter peaks is a long *arête* called the Knife Edge. Its almost sheer drop on both sides also has no counterpart in the Appalachians. West and north of Baxter Peak is a large sloping plateau called the Tableland. And at the NE side of the huge horseshoe is barren Hamlin Ridge.

Beyond Hamlin Ridge to the north is a second cirque, though not as large, called the North Basin. Further north is a third, even smaller cirque, the Little North Basin.

Chimney Pond, a small mountain tarn, is located in the floor of the Great Basin. It is a spectacular as well as ideal place to base one's climbs around the basin. Most of the mountain is above tree line, adding to its attractiveness.

These and many other features tend to draw the bulk of the Park's visitors to this area.

There are only two major trunk trails in the area: the Russell Pond Trail leading north to the central part of the Park, and the Chimney Pond Trail leading up to the floor of the Great Basin from Roaring Brook Campground. The other trails in the area form a network of short paths to various features previously mentioned. This provides an almost unlimited variety of possible loop trips on the mountain.

There are also trails to South Turner Mt., Sandy Stream Pond, and Katahdin Lake included in this section.

The Chimney Pond Trail   3.3 mi.

This is the main feeder trail to reach all the other trails around the Great Basin, as well as the connector trail between Roaring Brook and Chimney Pond campgrounds. It is heavily used. It follows an old tote road west, ascending along Roaring Brook to Basin Ponds. There used to be an old lumber camp here but it is long gone. Only an open clearing marks its existence. However, remains of the water-control dam at the pond's outlet may still be seen. The trail then climbs into the Great Basin through the horseshoe opening and ends at the campground. The total elevation gained is a moderate 1,425 ft. The ascent time is approx. 2³/₄ hours, the descent one hour less.

The trail is blue-blazed and has **ample water** so none need be carried.

Ascent Mileage

**Trail Data
Chimney Pond Trail**

0.0
mi.   At a prominent signpost near the ranger's cabin at Roaring Brook Campground, proceed past cabin (left) on trail. In 25 yds. pass second cabin (right) and reach junction of trails. **Chimney Pond Trail bears left** and parallels Roaring Brook upstream along old tote road. To right **Russell Pond Trail** crosses Roaring Brook and leads 7.1 mi. to that pond in the central part of the Park. 100 yds. further, the **Helon Taylor Trail** branches left, leading 3.2 mi. to Pamola Peak.

1.1   Cross bridge over large brook whch is the outlet of Pamola Pond (located near the base of Pamola Peak). Ascend moderately ahead.

2.0   Reach open area near shore of Basin Pond (elev. 2,447

An excellent panorama of Chimney Pond.

ft.). To right along shore of pond is an old lumberman's dam on pond's outlet. Basin Ponds are actually a string of three ponds (the uppermost is called Depot Pond) of which only the lower is seen from the trail. The views of the ridges, cirques, and mountain peaks above this point are truly outstanding. The trail follows the south and west shores of the pond.

2.2   Leave shore of pond and bear left (west) ascending steadily uphill into the mouth of the Great Basin.

2.3   Pass on right, **North Basin Cut-off** leading 0.7 mi. to the North Basin Trail. Continue ahead, crossing a number of brooks on log bridges.

2.7   Pass on right a depression in a glacial moraine called Dry Pond. This holds water in the spring or after a heavy rain, but soon drains bone dry.

2.9   Cross brook on log bridge and ascend more gradually.

3.0   Reach trail junction. **To right is North Basin Trail** which leads to Hamlin Ridge, Blueberry Knoll, and the North Basin.

3.2   Pass bunkhouse on left at edge of campground.

3.3   Reach ranger's cabin at trail's end in sight of Chimney Pond. To left is the **Dudley Trail** and to right are the **Cathedral and Saddle trails.** Elevation of pond is 2,914 ft.

Descent Mileage	Trail Data Chimney Pond Trail

0.0   Leave ranger's cabin near shore of Chimney Pond and
mi.   proceed east away from pond passing through campground, soon beginning gradual descent through conifers.

0.3   Reach trail junction. To left is **North Basin Trail** which leads to Hamlin Ridge, Blueberry Knoll, and the North Basin.

0.4   Cross brook on log bridge and descend more steeply out of Great Basin.

Descent Mileage

Trail Data
Chimney Pond Trail (cont.)

0.6 mi.   Pass on left a depression in a glacial moraine called Dry Pond. This holds water in the spring or after a heavy rain, but soon drains bone dry. Cross several brooks ahead.

1.0   Pass on left **North Basin Cut-off** leading 0.7 mi. to the North Basin Trail.

1.1   Reach west shore of Lower Basin Pond and follow around west and south shores.

1.3   Reach open area near shore of Basin Pond. Elevation here is 2,447 ft. To left along shore of pond is an old lumberman's dam on pond's outlet. Basin Ponds is actually a string of three ponds (the uppermost is called Depot Pond) of which only the lower is seen from the trail. Beyond pond begin moderate descent following old tote road.

2.2   Cross bridge over large brook which is the outlet of Pamola Pond (located near the base of Pamola Peak). Cross several smaller brooks ahead.

2.7   Reach south bank of Roaring Brook and continue to parallel downstream.

3.3   After passing junction with **Helon Taylor Trail** coming in on right, and **Russell Pond Trail** coming in on left, reach trail's end at edge of parking lot at Roaring Brook Campground. Ranger's camp is to right.

Russell Pond Trail   7.1 mi.

This trail provides the shortest access from a road to the central part of the Park and Russell Pond Campground. It is primarily a valley trail crossing several low ridges. It leaves Roaring Brook Campground and proceeds north through a wide valley between part of Katahdin and Russell Mt. to the west and south, and North Turner Mt. to the east. It then crosses wide Wassataquoik Stream and ends at Russell Pond.

An alternate route to reach Russell Pond is to follow the Russell Pond Trail for 3.3 mi., then branch off down the South Branch of the Wassataquoik following the **Tracy Horse Trail**, which rejoins the Russell Pond Trail 0.4 mi. south of Russell Pond. This route is more scenic and is only 0.4 mi. longer than the Russell Pond Trail. It does require a long ford across Wassataquoik Stream which could be dangerous in high water. See data for Tracy Horse Trail.

The Russell Pond Trail has **ample water** so none need be carried. It is blue-blazed. Estimated hiking time is 5 hours with full packs.

The trail data here are given only from south to north (Roaring Brook to Russell Pond). For data in opposite direction, see description of this trail in the "Central Park Trails" section.

Trail Data

| Mileage | **Russell Pond Trail** |

| 0.0 mi. | Trail leaves parking lot at Roaring Brook Campground near ranger's cabin (left). Follow well-worn path past cabin for 50 yds. to trail junction just beyond second cabin. **Russell Pond Trail turns right** and immediately crosses Roaring Brook on bridge. To left is **Chimney Pond Trail.** |

Fifty yds. beyond bridge, **Russell Pond Trail turns sharp left.** Ahead is **Sandy Stream Pond Trail** which rejoins the Russell Pond Trail 1.0 mi. further north.

0.4	Pass on right, small beaver flowage. Ascend gradually through hardwoods. Cross large brook at 0.5 mi.
1.1	Reach northern junction of Sandy Stream Pond Trail (comes in on right).
1.3	Come in sight of south end of Whidden Pond and skirt east shore.

Trail Data

Mileage

1.4 mi. Pass on left a short, side trail leading to shore of Whidden Pond. This gives the best view on this trail, with the entire east side of Katahdin and its great cirques visible. Elevation here is 1,619 ft. Trail ahead follows shore for short distance, then bears NE away from pond slabbing a flank of South Turner Mt. and passing through a hardwood forest.

3.2 Descend to the South Branch of the Wassataquoik and swing onto old tote road.

3.3 Reach trail junction. **Russell Pond Trail turns left** and leaves tote road. To right is the **Tracy Horse Trail** which continues down the South Branch to its confluence with the main Wassataquoik Stream, then rejoins the Russell Pond Trail 0.4 mi. south of Russell Pond.

3.4 Cross the South Branch of Wassataquoik.

3.6 Cross branch of main stream on small bridge. Beyond, ascend gradually.

3.8 Pass around and under an unusually shaped, house-sized boulder. The wide overhang of this boulder can provide temporary shelter from heavy summer showers. Beyond, trail climbs around and over a rocky shoulder of Russell Mt. (to left). High cliffs are seen through trees.

4.8 Cross large brook, then several smaller ones ahead. Continue to contour around the northeast side of Russell Mt. through a beautiful grove of mature hardwoods. Trail gradually descends into the Wassataquoik Valley.

6.5 Reach wide Wassataquoik Stream and follow downstream a short distance. Cross stream on two high log bridges anchored in midstream to an island. This stream drains a large area and is dangerous in high water. Beyond bridges, bear away from stream.

6.7 Reach trail junction with **Tracy Horse Trail** (to right). This leads east into fields which were a part of the New